CREATING
A NEW GARDEN

For Dominic and Josh Whiten

CREATING A NEW GARDEN

FAITH & GEOFF WHITEN

W·W·Norton & Company
New York·London

© Faith and Geoffrey Whiten 1986

First American edition, 1986

W. W. Norton & Company, Inc., 500 Fifth Avenue, New York, NY 10110.
W. W. Norton & Company, Ltd., 37 Great Russell Street, London WC1B 3NU.

Originally published in 1986 by Bell & Hyman Ltd, London.

ISBN 0-393-02350-8

Designed by Elizabeth Palmer

Original line artwork by Paul Saunders

Printed in Great Britain
1 2 3 4 5 6 7 8 9 0

CONTENTS

Many of the illustrations of gardens designed by Geoff and Faith Whiten that appear in this book were taken at the Royal Horticultural Society's Chelsea Show which is held each May in London. Their most recent exhibits have been on behalf of the Halifax Building Society – a cottage garden, a small city garden and especially two gardens for new homes. Through its involvement in the Chelsea Show and in other ways the Halifax has, more than any other building society, acknowledged the importance of gardens and it continues to recognise the significant contribution that a well landscaped garden can make to the benefits of home ownership and the general improvement of the environment.

ACKNOWLEDGEMENTS

We would very much like to thank the following people who have provided help and inspiration through their support in our various endeavours at the Chelsea Show, other shows and exhibitions and our own gardens – some of them for as long as twelve years.

Dick Spelman and his colleagues at the Halifax Building Society; Charles Notcutt and John Dyter of Notcutts Nurseries for their valued assistance in compiling the plant section of this book; Geoff Worrall, Pat Smit and David Wilkinson of Bradstone Garden Products; Alan Mitchell of Practical Woodworking magazine; Frederic Doerflinger of the International Flower Bulb Centre; Malcolm Pollard, sculptor and of course Elke; Jack McDavid formerly of Popular Gardening; Ray Waite of Wisely and Roy Lancaster for their advice on plants; Cliff Alcock and David Reed for their skill and craftsmanship, especially in stonework; Simon Dawes, Barry Holliman, Chris Thompson; Michael Chewter and Ray, Dominic and Josh and Win Colville for all their hard work.

Finally, for their photography we would like to thank Derek Goard, Graham Richardson and Heather Angel and for the use of photographs of their gardens Merrist Wood College, Peter Rogers, Douglas Knight, Preben Jakobsen and Telford Development Corporation.

FOREWORD

Another welcome book has come from the fertile and articulate pens of Faith and Geoff Whiten. It is aimed mainly at those who, possibly as first time buyers, move into a new house and are faced with the daunting task of making a new garden in the surrounding space, which probably still has some builders' rubble engrained in the soil. At the same time it is useful to those moving into a previously occupied house who find the garden so neglected or otherwise displeasing that they wish to start afresh. And for those whose own gardens are already well established this book is a source of inspiring ideas for modifying an existing layout, improving focal points or making detailed refinements.

It is also highly stimulating to look at for it is generously illustrated with plans, line drawings and colour photographs; these together with the text should help readers to apply the authors' principles and ideas to their own circumstances.

To the wide range of people to whom the subject of this book is relevant I recommend it unreservedly. It is well written and easy and agreeable to read. So much so that, although I have an old and extensive garden to look after and develop, I fantasised enjoyably when I read the book on how I could use the authors' ideas to make for myself a new small garden.

The Lord Aberconway,
President Emeritus,
The Royal Horticultural Society

1 First Thoughts

This book is about gardens—about creating a beautiful garden that is pleasing to look at and practical to use. But gardens do not exist in isolation; they tend to come attached to houses. When you buy a new house, you get a new garden and that almost invariably means an empty plot that needs filling rather desperately.

However, being realistic, it also means that this empty plot is demanding attention at just the same time as a long list of other jobs, both large and small, and so we have to put the garden into perspective as just one aspect of the whole process of uprooting children, pets and worldly goods and moving them to new surroundings in the hope of settling them as painlessly as possible.

It is hardly surprising that moving house has come to be acknowledged as one of the most stressful events in our lives. This must be due in part to the financial and legal negotiations which so often seem subject to endless delay, but also due to the fact that there is simply so much to organise; major to very minor decisions to be taken that are all, nevertheless, vitally important for the future.

Perhaps the most stressful element of all is change, and yet although changes in routine and surroundings can be the cause of strain, they can also be stimulating and satisfying in many ways. Of course, this is especially true if you have made a positive decision to move, but even if you have had changes thrust upon you it is hard to deny a sense of anticipation and even some excitement at the prospect of taking over a house that is new to you—more so if the house itself is brand new, and just waiting for you to breathe life and character into it.

These days, the chances are that a new house will have been slightly personalised to your taste before you move in, as so many builders offer a choice of colours and finishes in kitchen and bathroom fittings and general décor. Of course, as well as location and position, the design and finish of a house are strong factors that influence everybody's decision to buy. The general style of the exterior and the way in which the interior space is used are both important; surely everyone wants a smart, attractive finish combined with convenience and practicality. Most people, too, have an eye to the value of the property and the way in which that is likely to appreciate, proving a sound investment when it is time to move on again.

These are all the practical considerations that we have in mind when looking at houses, and they are just as relevant to gardens. The difference is that whilst very few builders would contemplate offering an unfinished house for sale, that is exactly what they almost always do with the garden, so the whole business of achieving a garden that is well designed and finished, which is an asset to the value and desirability of the house, is the responsibility of you, the buyer.

If the house you are buying is more mature, then it may be new to you but the garden is quite likely to have fallen into sad, overgrown neglect or to have passed through the hands of several owners, each with their own disparate ideas of what a garden should look like—and it shows. Although this introduction tends to highlight the particular problems of new home owners, it must not be thought that owners of established gardens will find nothing of use in the book. You may find too daunting the prospect of ripping out existing lawns, paths and borders and starting again completely, but ideas for the improvement of existing gardens are another matter. If you want to alter the hard line of a straight path or a lawn then the designs will certainly give help and guidance, and the Features and Plants sections have many ideas for building and decorating a new patio, as well as other ways of livening up specific areas of the garden and creating points of interest within the overall design.

Of course, life would probably be simpler if all decisions affecting our choice of where to live were made with the head, in the light of hard finances and practicalities, rather than the heart. But they are not, for the way in which we think about houses and gardens is—thank goodness—emotional as well as practical. No matter that the house doesn't really have enough room—just look at those delightful windows and the magnificent view from the lounge; the garden may be a jungle at present, but that old apple tree is so nice and there is so much that you could do with it . . . it has atmosphere we say, it feels right and so we buy now and later we rotovate, cultivate, plant, nurture and mow.

The fact that we are prepared to go to so much trouble emphasises a human reality—that gardens matter to people. Almost everyone with a family longs to have their own house with its own garden. Certainly the desire for our own domain—our exclusive small territory that is private and secure—must be acknowledged but it is also important to have open, outdoor space that can be shared and enjoyed with family and friends—somewhere to play games or just mess about, to have a bonfire, to work at planting and weeding or simply to wander round or sit on a warm summer's evening.

A garden also helps to keep us in touch with the natural world, in contrast to so much that is mechanical and mass-produced in our lives today. In towns and cities especially it reminds people of the natural rhythm of the seasons, and we derive pleasure and satisfaction from observing not only the early flowers of spring and the bright flourish of summer, but also autumn's berries and yellowing leaves and even the cold, bare twigs of winter as the whole cycle prepares to begin again.

Another very important benefit of gardens is that they help to determine the character of a house and lend to the property a sense of individuality. If the new house is a one-off, then it is quite likely to have some distinctive style or architectural characteristic and the garden should reflect that. The quiet sophistication of brown brick and dark stained timber deserves the lush, imposing foliage of evergreen shrubs, good-sized trees and a clean sweep of emerald lawn to complement its feel of quality, whereas a new house finished in 'traditional English style' with

These two gardens demonstrate that it is possible to create a beautiful setting, both in apparently awkward circumstances like a steep slope (right) and in an otherwise barren space like a rooftop (above). Both make dramatic use of sculptured figures set in water but rely on the cool, restful effect of greens, yellows and whites for their planting.

Both illustrate plants chosen for shape and texture to blend with structural materials — in one case, planed timber used in American style to make decking, steps and pergola and in the other York stone split to form thin, light-weight tiles. Gardens by the landscape students of Merrist Wood college; sculptures by David Norris.

white paint and beams demands a softer, prettier garden.

Style is probably rather an overworked word these days, but a garden *can* lend a house style and distinction. It can say something about the people who live there and, on a new housing development where all the houses look very similar, it can contribute a great deal towards giving the house a stamp of individuality.

A good garden that is unusual in an attractive, tasteful way makes a house stand out from its neighbours and can be an excellent selling feature, even adding value to the property. If a garden is reasonably well established, with good plants and features, and seems easy to maintain then buyers feel encouraged and reassured that they won't have the expense of laying out the garden from scratch, nor will they have to spend too much time and effort on its upkeep. This is widely acknowledged by estate agents and building societies, who find that where two or three similar properties are on the market in close proximity the one with a well landscaped garden will almost certainly sell first.

However, there are important reservations and exceptions. If a garden is too individual it can actually prove a deterrent to prospective buyers—if your taste runs, for instance, to a collection of gnomes and windmills perched beside rock pools or to a Union flag picked out in red, white and blue flowers the width of the front garden then it is quite possible that your garden will not be to everybody's taste and may well put some people off! Similarly, it rarely pays to add features that are too large for the size of the garden or too expensive for the immediate area and general level of property values. A swimming pool is a particular example; in the garden of an ordinary semi-detached or on the average housing development it can actually render the house and garden out of proportion with its neighbours and rarely proves a wise investment.

Quite aside from self-restraint, you may be forced to temper any extreme ambitions by restrictions imposed by the builder of a new development—this applies generally to front gardens rather than back, especially where the scheme is 'open plan' and therefore intended to form a clean sweep of driveways and lawns, softened perhaps by low planting or specimen trees and shrubs but uninterrupted by boundary fences, walls and hedges. If these are allowed at all, there is often a height restriction, as there may be on plants.

Even where no specific restrictions have been imposed on front gardens by the local authority planners or the developer, it is still desirable to have a sense of overall design and to be aware not only of what may be beneficial to the value of your property, but also what is considerate to the interests of others.

For instance, planners and developers often lay out houses in a group or a close, so that all the frontages combine to create a complete picture that has a sense of cohesion and unity. The width of the driveways is uniform and the line they take is part of the overall concept of the site layout; the remainder of the garden is often turfed. It is wise to be conscious that the frontage of your house forms part of this overall vista; often it is pleasing to see touches of individuality in the form of attractive planting, a feature by the front door and even a modest and fairly unobtrusive addition to the drive for turning or to provide an extra car standing space. But, if your frontage is altered too drastically, then it can jar when seen in too stark a contrast to its surroundings and actually becomes less attractive.

Not that we would advocate making no improvements or alterations whatsoever to the front garden, for it is the public face of the house and creates important first impressions. There are ideas in this book for features that can enhance and enliven front gardens and for layouts that make the front of the house both attractive and more practical, with room to park the car and walk to the front door without getting muddy feet or with the introduction of an enlarged step to the door with a feature plant bed or pool, making it more imposing and welcoming.

It is nevertheless in the back garden that there is perhaps most opportunity for individualisation, although you may see the back garden as more of a burden than an opportunity! Depending on your point of view, the creation of a new garden is either a challenge on which you cannot

These details of gardens designed by Peter Rogers all demonstrate the cheerful colour and softening effect that varied shrub planting can lend to a garden. In addition, each has something to say about garden features. The graceful combination of fountain and dragonfly sculpture would be a delightful focal point seen through a window at any time of year and the striking gazebo makes a pleasant place to sit in all but the coldest weather. An unusual way of dealing with a change of level in a sloping site is demonstrated by the curved retaining wall and circular paving. A bushy, low-growing subject (in this case Tolmeia) makes good cover at the base of the wall.

wait to get started, or an enormous, frightening chore that you keep putting off until it will wait no longer.

Of course, one quite valid reason for delaying the whole business may be that you simply don't know where to start or even exactly what you are starting to do. That is where this book is intended to help—to offer ideas and guidance so that you can embark on the creation of a beautiful garden with a sense of purpose.

On a new housing development it is quite common to observe recently settled householders (and, on most, it is possible to see them all too clearly!) go out into the garden and look around, scratching their heads in despair and bewilderment. They dig about a bit half-heartedly, move soil from one place to another and put down a couple of planks to span the muddiest parts and reach the rotary clothes dryer, and then they go back indoors until the next weekend which hopefully will be wet.

If that has a familiar ring, then it may be some comfort to know that you are not alone, for most new houses present very much the same selection of problems and requirements when it comes to that wasteland that is laughingly called a garden.

The main obvious problem is that there is nothing there. The house appears so stark rising out of this patch of bare earth, and seems desperately to need plants in order to soften its appearance and blend it into the surroundings. If it is a one-off or a group of three or four built in what had once been a mature site, then you might be fortunate enough to inherit mature trees and shrubs, so that there is already some sense of shelter and features to work around. However, on larger developments there is quite often nothing left in the garden; the area is just graded, possibly with topsoil added, and surrounded by a post and wire or chain link fence.

This tends to create the second major problem, which is lack of privacy. Every time you poke your head out of the back door you get that goldfish bowl feeling, for you are open to the view of all the neighbours and just as you may not want to be seen all the time you are pottering in the garden, so you may prefer not to have to observe them—it can be quite embarrassing.

The third problem is, in addition to lack of visual shelter, the lack of physical shelter, leaving the garden exposed to wind and completely lacking in shade other than that cast by the house itself. Although it's pleasant to have a light, sunny site, especially if you like really warm weather and enjoy sunbathing, it's worth remembering that many people—particularly babies and older people—benefit from a dappled shade rather than the full heat and glare of the sun, so it is desirable to introduce some form of shelter into the garden—perhaps with trees, a hedge or shrub planting.

This will have the additional benefit of acting as a windbreak, for it is unwise to underestimate the extent to which a strong cross-breeze can spoil your enjoyment whilst sitting in the garden—and in winter really cold winds can make it a completely hostile environment that puts you off even setting foot outside the back door. The problem is, of course, increased if you happen to live in a fairly high spot or coastal district, where windbreaks become even more vital.

Another practical problem is that of actually getting about the garden when it consists of nothing but brickbat-strewn soil which is sodden and squelchy for most of the winter and hard and dusty in a hot, dry, summer.

At the very least you will need a path to enable you to move around the garden—even if it's only to hang out the washing—without stepping up to the ankles in mud, which inevitably treads indoors. In addition to a path most people would want the garden to include some form of clean ground surfacing for sitting outside, for children's play and for storage—all of which are unpleasant and inconvenient when the plot consists of nothing but rough soil.

The condition of the soil itself may well be yet another problem to be dealt with before it is possible to grow plants that will offer a pleasing and changing pattern of flowers and folliage throughout the year. Plants ideally need soil that allows water to drain away rather than form a waterlogged mess, but not so quickly that the nutrients in the soil are

The site is level and neatly finished, but there is an urgent need for hard surfacing to make the garden accessible and for planting to soften the house and garage.

A small garden planned with ornamental interest in mind.

Decorative paving, stone chippings and pebbles all create a rich variety of ground textures, and there are even hollow plastic 'pebbles' floating on the pond. Glazed earthenware Chinese pots and an elegant wooden bridge with ornate details give the garden an oriental feel.

Planting is in bold groups and combines familiar ivies, lilies and rhododendrons with more exotic plants like the spiky, silver leaved Astelia in the foreground; tiny grass-like Caryx with cream variegation growing amongst boulders and the bold, deep green foliage of Pseudopanax 'Cyril Watson' to the right of the large urn. (All thrive in a mild climate or sheltered position).
Design by Geoff and Faith Whiten in association with the Halifax Building Society. Bridge design by Ashley Cartwright with Practical Woodworking magazine.

washed away before they have a chance to do any good.

At this stage it is worth mentioning that whatever the type of soil in a new garden, it is likely to be littered with brickbats and general building debris which should, of course, be removed. Even when good loose topsoil has been spread by the builder so that the garden seems ready for planting, you may find that under the surface the ground is still very hard and compacted—often the effect of heavy machinery used on site—and to encourage good drainage you just have to dig deeply and thoroughly.

If the garden has a really serious drainage problem, to the extent that paths are flooded when it rains, then it is wise to refer back to the house builder's after-sales service to see whether it is necessary to install land drains and whether the builders will undertake this as part of their obligations.

To return to the problems for which you must try to find solutions, those that we have described are probably most common and most tiresome although, of course, every site has its own idiosyncracies and not all garden owners have the same needs and priorities.

Nevertheless, we have found that the process of transforming a depressing wasteland into an inviting setting for outdoor living can be approached most effectively and most logically in three stages. The first is to establish a basic ground plan for the layout of the garden and so the Designs section offers ideas in plan form for gardens of a wide range of shapes and sizes.

The second stage, having established the bones of the actual design, is to add some flesh in the form of features—not only practical basic items like paths, patios, lawns and play areas but also more ornamental attractions like a pond, waterfall, rock feature, sculpture, pots and outdoor lighting. These eminently achievable ideas, contained in the Features section, are just as important as the more functional aspects of the garden and, with a little flair, can actually raise the creation of a new garden into a decorative art form.

The third vital stage is the introduction of plants that are suitable for the site and which, as well as looking beautiful, will best fulfil a necessary function like casting shade, softening a fence, screening from neighbours or making a carpet of ground cover. Our final section on Plants lists specimens ranging from trees to miniature bulb flowers, indicating which are suitable for particular soils, positions and purposes.

The fact that several months may elapse after moving into a new house before you are actually ready to embark on these three stages of making the garden can prove beneficial, for you will have had time to get to know the place and to assess its advantages and disadvantages. It will be useful to know which parts of the garden are sunny at various times of the day, which aspects are pleasant—not only in the garden itself but also the view from the lounge or dining room and the view from the kitchen as you stand at the sink or worktop.

It is also useful to establish which boundaries are your responsibility and to get the measure of your neighbours. It is, after all, only human to discover that you become the best of friends with the neighbours on one side, but cannot wait to put up a good high fence to screen from those on the other!

Thinking through the three stages of design, features and plants is beneficial not only because you will create a more successful garden, but also because it enables you to work towards a specific end result. This makes economic sense in terms of both time and money and should help to avoid a great deal of possible frustration.

As regards finance, there are several alternative approaches. You may decide to buy the necessary tools, materials and plants as and when funds permit, carrying out the work yourself and completing it over a period of time. In order to speed up the early, rather messy stages and to make the garden at least usable fairly quickly, you might prefer to prepare the site and install paving, boundary fences or hedges, turf and a basic framework of plants initially, adding more interesting features and more varied planting at a slower pace.

Finally, you may have the capital to complete the creation of the new garden in one fell swoop or consider raising sufficient finance to do so. This is increasingly available from building societies who are willing to consider loans for landscaping, in addition to mortgages, in recognition of the asset of a well landscaped garden to the overall value of the property. Access to capital finance then offers the choice of doing the work yourself or calling on help from a professional landscaper or company, even if it is only to carry out the heavier 'construction' work of paving, walling, steps, fencing and so on, leaving you to plant and add the finishing touches.

Opposite: The curved
brickwork is a pleasing
feature here. It retains the
raised pond, lush planted
areas and sloping lawn
but also acts as a clever
design device, leading the
eye to the garden room —
an inviting place to sit
and take in a different
view of the garden.

Design by David Stevens
for Woolworths.
In contrast, a tiny garden
(above) relies for interest
on small details rather
than the broad sweep.
The Buddha lends an
eye-catching sense of
mystery under the
window box.

2 Designs

Design matters in gardens. The basic layout of the site is a vital starting point and yet it is unrealistic to expect everyone who moves into a new house and garden to become a designer overnight. Even knowledgeable gardening friends—some of them professional growers—have been known to invite us for lunch or a weekend, adding the casual suggestion that while we are there perhaps we could tell them what to do with the garden.

That, of course, is the great question. What to do with the garden? You may not even know what you want to include until you have seen something that sparks off an idea, and it is certainly not easy to see how to treat a plot in terms of the line of the layout, especially if the site is steeply sloping or awkwardly shaped. Design is not just a question of what to include, but also where to put all the features and how to tie them together in a layout that is harmonious and pleasing to the eye, is well balanced and introduces a sense of purpose as well as a good overall shape.

We have found from the experience of friends and neighbours that the most difficult aspect of creating a new garden is that first step of determining some kind of initial groundplan. Almost anybody can make a garden that consists of a square of paving by the back door, a lawn and a straight border around the edge, but most people nowadays quite rightly aspire to something a little more sophisticated. Besides, that basic layout is all very well if the garden has a regular rectangular shape, but what if the boundary runs at a series of odd angles, if you have a corner plot that goes around the side of the house, if the site runs level then sharply falls or raises, if the plot is long and narrow or wedge-shaped? What if it is dominated by an existing feature like a row of mature trees?

Builders increasingly succeed in using every last scrap of valuable land on a housing development and now tend to plan a more attractive and informal layout in contrast to the old straight rows of houses that make up so many suburban streets. However, random groups around 'village greens' and small cul-de-sacs mean that householders often find themselves with a plot that at its simplest is more square than rectangular and can be almost totally random in shape.

So, we have taken as the starting point for our series of designs plots of differing shape and size and the various problems likely to be encountered. The plans are intended to give ideas and guidelines that are bold and interesting in style and yet at the same time practical and achievable for ordinary householders. They should help to make the best possible use of a site and to compensate for its faults and shortcomings. The actual style of the various plans is intentionally not diverse, for we hope that they will be read as a collection which features some of the distinctive design characteristics that we have developed over the years, and which

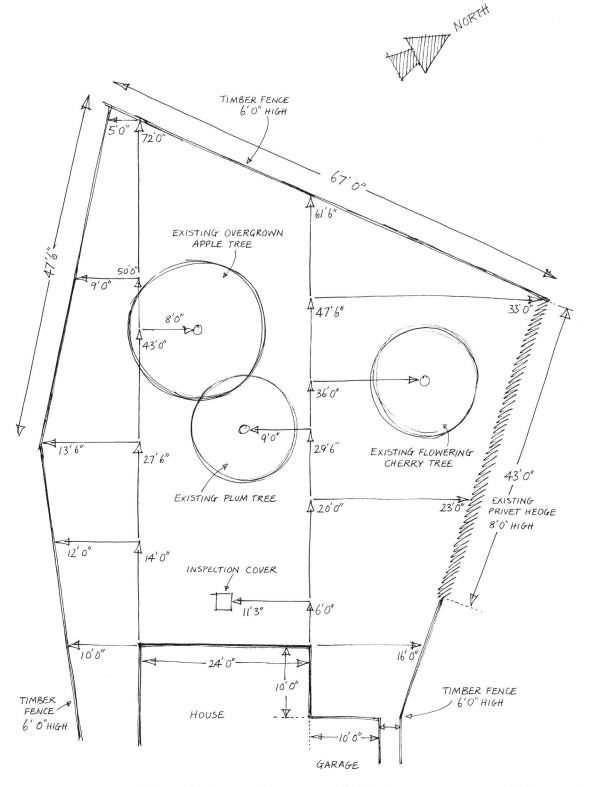

NORTH

TIMBER FENCE
6'0" HIGH

EXISTING OVERGROWN
APPLE TREE

5'0"

72'0"

67'0"

61'6"

47'6"

50'6"

9'0"

47'6"

8'0"

43'0"

33'0"

36'0"

9'0"

EXISTING FLOWERING
CHERRY TREE

13'6"

27'6"

29'6"

43'0"

EXISTING PLUM TREE

EXISTING
PRIVET HEDGE
8'0" HIGH

12'0"

14'0"

20'0"

23'0"

INSPECTION COVER

11'3"

6'0"

10'0"

16'0"

24'0"

10'0"

TIMBER FENCE
6'0" HIGH

TIMBER
FENCE
6'0" HIGH

HOUSE

10'0"

GARAGE

Measure firstly across the back of the house, plotting its exact position by marking in the corners. Run string the length of the garden in a line at right angles to the rear wall of the house. Along this line mark off at intervals, measuring across the width of the garden at a right angle to plot strategic points of the site boundary and permanent features such as trees. This basic, simple survey may not result in exact accuracy, but a discrepancy of up to 6 in or so is hardly likely to cause problems.

Ornamental features can make a patio area, but they should blend and harmonise. The patio garden opposite combines Traditional walling and the tiled effect of Corinium paving, (both in a weathered York finish) with honey-coloured limestone chippings and larger pebbles in browns and greys. Planting is restrained, with only occasional colour highlights; specimens combine with ground cover for relative ease of maintenance. The timber bridge spans a long, narrow pool and matches the low table and benches.

Similarly, the raised pool above is finished in coping stones to blend with the paving and the smooth, 'stone' finish of the sculpted heads. Patio plants soften and blend the harder materials.

27

may be familiar to anybody who has seen our regular exhibits at the Chelsea Show or elsewhere. Nevertheless, our aim has been to present ideas that are sufficiently flexible to cater for a range of tastes.

There are several features common to most designs—probably most notably a paved area of generous proportions set either square with the house or at an angle to it. There are, too, many stepping stone paths and their function of providing access is often secondary to their role in balancing the design and helping to give it shape—even an additional ornamental quality. Of course, stepping stones set in grass create work, but this can be greatly eased if they are set slightly below the finished lawn level and a hover type of mower is used for cutting. Equally, when translating the design it is possible to adapt them to create continuous paths.

For ease and continuity of drafting, all the paving slabs indicated are approximately 2 × 2 ft (600 by 600 mm) in size, but the actual module of paving is, in fact, almost infinitely variable within the outline of the paved areas shown. Indeed, in a small garden a smaller module or a slab which creates the effect of bricks, tiles or sets can be more complementary to the overall scale.

We have not made specific recommendations for boundary fencing because your requirements will obviously depend on what is provided on the site and the degree of privacy needed. Most likely existing boundaries will be of brick walls, timber fence panels, post and wire or chain link fencing. However, where screen or baffle walls are indicated within the design, rather than on the boundary, these would normally be constructed from brick or ornamental garden walling blocks to a height of 6 ft (1.8 m) or 6 ft 6 in (2 m) and to a thickness of 9 in (22 cm).

Some features common to most of the plans need not be taken too literally; their detailed character is less important than their shape, size and position. Many include a square pool, which could be at ground level or slightly raised and finished with a fountain. However, this could equally be a feature bed for herbs or flowering plants, a timber deck for lounging or a paved plinth for planted pots. Indeed, we cannot emphasise too strongly the need for care and safety concerning children and water. If there are children under, say, seven years old who regularly use the garden then you should go for one of the 'dry' alternatives or perhaps a submersible pump concealed under pebbles to create a bubble fountain which simply splashes continuously over the stones without forming an expanse of water.

These are just some practical pointers towards using the designs, and you will find more details of what can be included in the Features section. As regards their shape, we have aimed to incorporate clean, simple lines that are easy to translate from paper into the actual garden setting. The notes and diagrams on surveying the site and marking out give a guide, and do remember that getting out in the garden to see how the design might fit can be very much more illuminating than endlessly fussing with pencil and paper. If you have a house rather than a bungalow, the best way to get a sense of the shape and proportions of the garden is to look down from the upstairs windows. One person might mark the proposed layout with sand or string lines while another guides and comments from upstairs. Although some patience may be necessary to prevent this operation from prompting a fierce argument, you might be quite pleasantly surprised as shapes that looked too large or bold on plan start to make sense when seen *in situ*, and the way in which a plan can be adapted or adjusted to fit your particular plot could fall readily into place.

It is obviously fortunate if a plan suits your garden almost exactly or can readily be adapted to fit, but we hope that these designs will be useful even if they only present ideas that you may not have previously considered—something as simple as the angle of the patio, the curve of a border or the generous proportion of features and lack of fussy detail.

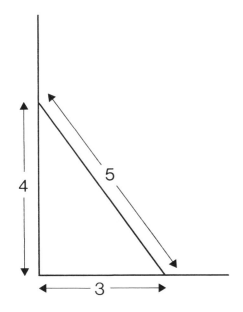

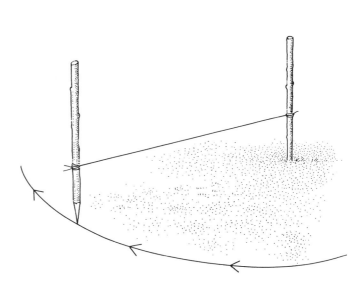

For ease of marking out, many of our designs include curved shapes that are formed by straight lines with rounded corners. Two basic shapes—a right angle and a curve—are particularly useful if set accurately; from these other lines of the design will more readily fall into place.

To set a right angle (above, left) use string and pegs to form a triangle of the dimensions shown (or multiples of these). The right angle is at the point where the shorter sides meet.

To form a curve (above, right) use two sticks with string on the principle of a compass, one to fix in the ground and the other to move freely in an arc, scratching out a groove which can be dug out with a spade or marked with a line of sand. A short length of string makes a tight, small curve, and a longer length a large, more sweeping curve.

The overall design is set at an angle, creating greater flexibility and a sense of movement in its lines.

Shape is obviously important but it is perhaps the details that really make the garden, from the simple group of iris to the casually arranged boulders and pebbles or the occasional cushions which blend with plant shades. The colours in their turn — pink, red, rust, gold, yellow, cream — create a feeling of warmth and harmony.

Design for a square shaped plot

If any garden can be described as typical, then it is fair to say that this plot is typical of many that belong to three or four bedroom detached or semi-detached houses on new developments. The site is level and is roughly square in shape, measuring approximately 40 ft by 40 ft (12 m × 12 m). To one side of the house is a fairly wide access with a side gate towards the front and an existing concrete path leading around to the back door. The garage is attached to the house but there is no means of access from the kitchen or lounge to the back of the garage, for the narrow concrete path was the only existing feature of the garden.

This would have been difficult to remove and, in any case, most of the drain inspection covers are located in its vicinity, so the path is retained and framed with 'brick on edge' set at ground level. The main line of the design then takes the end of the path as its starting point and, for greater interest and flexibility, is set at an angle of 45 degrees to the house.

A paved patio offers room to sit outside as well as hard surface access from kitchen to garage. Its main feature is a patio pool, which could be set at ground level or raised—either to the height of one brick or to 18 in (45 cm). Alternatively, there could be a herb bed used for seasonal displays of bulbs or summer bedding.

The central feature of the garden is an open area of either lawn or a surface of shingle or stone chippings softened by clumps of low-growing ground cover plants (see suggestions in Plants section); this would reduce maintenance in the garden as a whole to a minimum. The area is framed by paving slabs creating a path system which runs almost right around the garden and could be handy for toddlers with tricycles. Both these paths and the brick edging to the border on the left hand side of the garden could also be softened by low growing plants to the front of the borders, tumbling over the edge and blurring the outline.

The far right hand corner of the garden is a good position for a new tree, which will give shelter and interest above eye level as well as providing a focal point. The base is partly surrounded by paving and a tree seat could be positioned here, offering a secluded place to sit and a different view of the garden, looking back towards the house itself.

In the left hand corner is a more utilitarian area. This might be a small vegetable plot, a storage area with a shed, a greenhouse and cold frame, a children's play area with or without a garden room or summerhouse—it really depends on the purpose for which you want to use the garden. In any event, this utility area is screened from the rest of the garden by a long, fairly narrow bed which could contain shrub planting or, say, climbing roses supported by a simple trellis. A selection for this, together with shrubs for the plant borders can be made from the various lists in the Plants section and again your choice is likely to depend not only on the soil and conditions but also how much actual gardening you want to do—whether you want a varied pattern of shrubs, perennials, annuals and bulbs or prefer to settle for basic shrubs that will take care of themselves as far as possible.

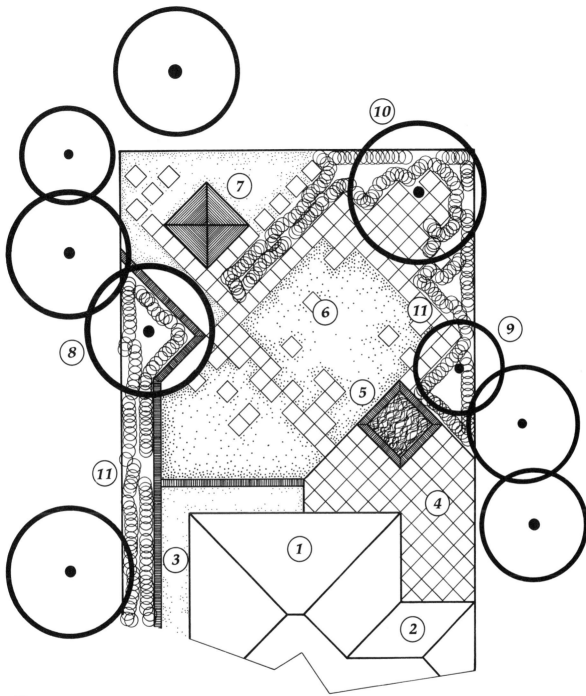

Key:

1. *Rear of house*
2. *Rear of garage*
3. *Existing concrete path enhanced by new brick edging extended to frame plant border*
4. *Paved patio set to angle*
5. *Patio pool or herb bed with brick surround*
6. *Lawn or shingled area with path system and paved area beneath existing tree*
7. *Utility or play area with shed/summerhouse screened by shrub planting*
8. *New fruit tree*
9. *New small weeping tree*
10. *Existing silver birch tree (Betula pendula) with tree seat and ground cover planting*
11. *Planted borders*

One sculpted figure, two different moods.
Formed in terracotta and set on a plinth in an open area framed by high walls the pair of figures has a sense of flowing rhythm when viewed from any direction and creates a lively focal point.
Cold cast in bronze and set at ground level against an ornamental timber screen, she is still fascinating, yet seems more restful, blending into the surrounding plants, paving and pebbles.
Garden designs by Geoff and Faith Whiten; Sculpture by Malcolm Pollard.

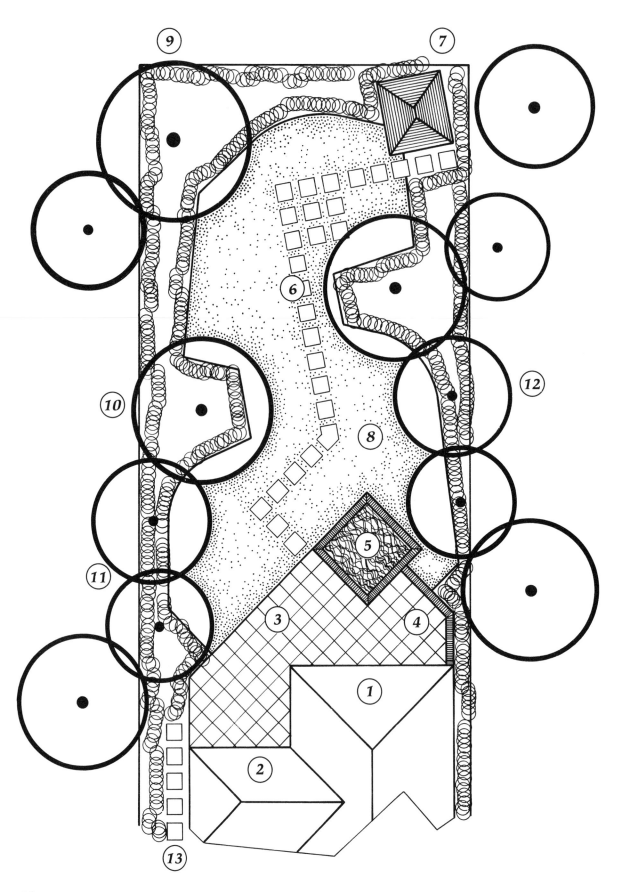

Simple design for a small, level, rectangular site

Not every garden has problems or complications, and this design might best be summed up as a simple layout for a straightforward site. The plot is basically level and takes the form of a regular rectangle. The house is detached and when brand new its garden featured only a small square of slabs outside the patio doors.

These slabs could be taken up and re-used either as stepping stones or to form part of the spacious patio, which runs across the width of the rear of the house and garage, giving plenty of space for a table and chairs and for the expanse of paving to be softened by several planted pots. For privacy and shelter from wind, the area is screened on the right hand side by a section of walling 6 ft (1.8 m) high; this too should be softened by planting—this time climbers, which can either be grown in containers or in beds formed by leaving out the occasional paving slabs adjacent to the wall.

At the corner of the patio is a raised pool. If you have small children or prefer not to include water, then this could equally be a raised bed planted with alpines and miniature conifers set amongst shingle and two or three pieces of rock. In either case, it provides a focal point when seen from the house or the patio.

Access to the front of the house is by stepping stones set in shingle and ground cover planting (for suggestions see appropriate list in Plants section). A second stepping stone path leads through the lawn to the far end of the garden; this is not only functional but acts as an important element of the design, bringing together the various angles of the patio and borders. It leads to a small garden building which could be a storage shed, chalet or children's room.

The plant borders follow interesting lines and yet they do not create vast areas to be planted. Indeed, the selection of small to medium sized trees indicated could be chosen to offer a variety of seasonal interest of foliage, berries and blossoms and then simply underplanted with shade-tolerant ground cover or evergreen subjects like azaleas and rhododendrons. The final result would be a garden that is lush and green with seasonal flashes of colour and yet very easy to care for.

This is, too, a layout that can be reduced to absolute basics for those who want to start along very economical lines, for it would be possible to commence with the patio, lawn and tree planting and—perhaps a few months later—add the pool or feature bed, stepping stone path and garden room and finally plant the borders.

Key:

1. Rear of house
2. Rear of garage
3. Paved patio set to angle
4. Screen wall 6 ft (1.8 m) high
5. Raised patio pool or plant bed
6. Stepping stone path to bottom of garden
7. Small garden storage shed, chalet or children's room
8. Lawn area surrounded by planted beds
9. Existing tree
10. Existing tree
11. Group of 2 new trees
12. Group of 3 new trees
13. Stepping stone path to front of house

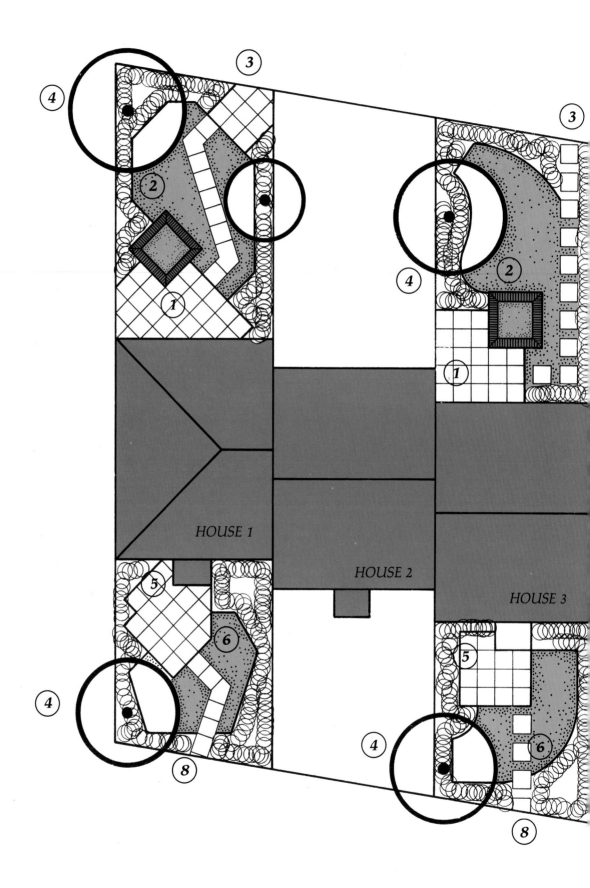

HOUSE 1

HOUSE 2

HOUSE 3

Variations on a theme for terraced houses

The layout of this row of small houses will be familiar to anybody who has browsed through plans of new housing developments. Usually referred to as town houses, cottages or starter homes, they range in size from four bedrooms on three stories to a compact two-up, two-down.

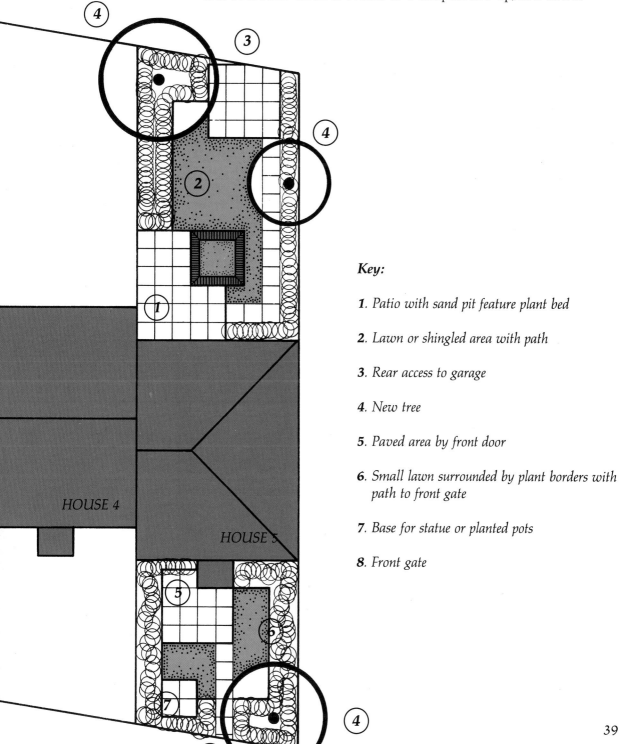

Key:

1. Patio with sand pit feature plant bed

2. Lawn or shingled area with path

3. Rear access to garage

4. New tree

5. Paved area by front door

6. Small lawn surrounded by plant borders with path to front gate

7. Base for statue or planted pots

8. Front gate

In tiny gardens space is at a premium, so every detail counts. Here, Corinium paving is laid to create five inter-locking circles with an open centre. It would be too obvious to position a pot right in the middle, so this glazed urn is set to one side. It stands on stone chippings and is complemented by pebbles that appear to be scattered at random. Ground hugging ivy completes the picture.

Many older terraces exist along similar lines, but these days the layout of the terrace is often slightly staggered—as the plan overleaf shows—to create a more varied and attractive frontage and afford a little more privacy. Also, as in this layout, there may be a gate at the bottom of the back garden to give access to the garage, located in a separate battery arrangement, or to a parking space.

The houses in this terrace have two bedrooms and are sold as starter homes primarily to singles, young couples and small families who tend to move on to something a bit bigger when a second child arrives. There are gardens front and back, but each is quite tiny and there is hardly room to achieve anything very elaborate—in any case an attractive but fairly utilitarian layout is likely to be a priority if resources are already stretched to make the repayments on a new home loan!

The three alternative 'front and back' designs are all variations on a simple theme, demonstrating that however small the space and however limited the resources it is possible to make an attractively shaped garden with a sense of style that raises it beyond the very basic and commonplace.

All three require similar components—basically a few paving slabs and bricks (the latter may be found when digging over the site—a legacy from the builder), some turf or grass or alternatively shingle, two or three small trees and some plants which might be herbaceous plants and annuals grown cheaply from seed or perhaps clumps from mature plants in the gardens of friends and relatives. In addition, some salad crops or fruit bushes may be planted. If there is a small child in the family, the square feature with brick edging in the back garden might be a sand pit or it could, alternatively, make a raised seat or a herb bed handy for the kitchen—again the plants can be grown from seed.

The designs for the front and back gardens of number one in the terrace are set at an angle, creating a lively shape with quite a modern, dynamic feel. Number three has a more gentle outline based on squares combined with pleasing curves and would perhaps be a good choice for anyone who enjoys growing soft, old-fashioned flowers like lupins, pinks, sweet William and pansies. Number five features a combination of solid squares and rectangles. These front and back layouts are perhaps the most simple to achieve and, if shingle or stone chippings were used as an alternative to grass, would require very little maintenance.

The 'site plan' here demonstrates clearly the extent to which the occupants of these houses are living at close quarters with their neighbours and our plans bring home not only the possibilities for 'doing your own thing' but also the benefits that can be enjoyed by some neighbourly co-operation (and transversely the problems that non-co-operation can cause!) The occupants of number two, for instance, hardly need to plant any trees as the branches of the trees in numbers one and three will overhang their garden. Number four, on the other hand, might plant a tree just below mid-way on their left hand boundary; this would benefit the gardens of both three and four without conflicting with existing planting.

In the city, gardens are especially important, offering a quiet, green environment as a haven from bustle, noise, traffic fumes and buildings that are harsh or drab in appearance. In this city garden there is hardly space for a grand sweep of design, but the details demonstrate what can be done. Octavian paving is chosen to complement brickwork; there are planted pots, window boxes and occasional stools. Many of the plants (hostas, ferns, mahonia, Fatsia japonica, rhododendrons) are tolerant of shady conditions and shrubs are combined with colourful bulb flowers, which can be allowed to naturalise as a permanent feature of the planted areas.

Garden designed by Geoff and Faith Whiten in association with the Halifax Building Society,

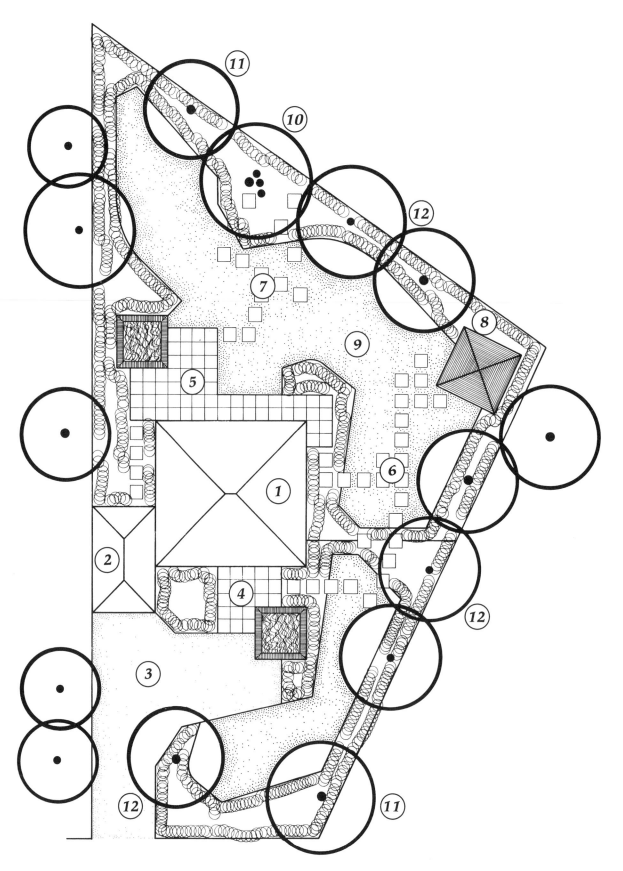

Design for front and back gardens in an odd-shaped plot

Not all new houses have tiny gardens; this bungalow with integral garage was built on a medium sized plot for a couple whose children had grown up and left home. Although it is nicely spacious and quite level, the plot nevertheless presented some design problems common to many irregularly shaped sites, whatever their scale.

The bungalow is situated well inside the plot and the basic philosophy behind the design is therefore that the front and back gardens should be treated not as two completely separate entities, but should be united and harmonised in an overall design, so that they link and blend in both shape and character. In plan form the overall pattern can be clearly seen, as if from the air, but even at ground level one would be conscious of the satisfying sense of a design theme followed through, creating a more successful garden with a pleasing thoughtfulness and attention to detail.

The object of the design for the front garden is to make the whole house frontage smart, imposing and ornamental, even though the bungalow itself is quite small—just the sort of impression that would add to its value and desirability. With this in mind, the front door step is extended to form a paved area sheltered by an overhead pergola. To the left hand side is shrub planting, which could take the form of ground cover around a statue, and to the right a small square pool which could, again, be a feature plant bed; this area would be an ideal location for an exterior light to cast a soft glow across the driveway.

The drive itself is adequate for one car's width at the entrance so that most of the frontage can be screened from the road by a border of trees and shrubs. Inside the plot, it opens up, but not so greatly as to dominate the front garden; you might say there is just enough space for the company car to enter the garage and a small runabout to pull up outside the front door step!

A stepping stone path links the front with the rear garden, and the stepping stones themselves are set in a pleasing pattern amongst planting as well as in grass. In the back, many of the themes established to the front of the house are echoed and expanded. Again, the paved area is set square to the house; again it features a square pool or plant bed and could also be finished with a pergola.

The line of the borders is another continuing theme, creating what might be called straightened curves. Although they make for an unusually shaped lawn, they utilise the odd-shaped plot to the full, fitting neatly into and complementing its outline rather than trying to fight it. In the right hand corner a gazebo or garden room makes a pleasant place to sit in this spacious garden with its strong sense of design harmony and flow.

Key:

1. *Bungalow*
2. *Garage*
3. *Drive area*
4. *Paved front door area (set square to building) with small pool or feature plant bed*
5. *Paved patio area with small pool or feature plant bed and stepping stone path through planting to rear of garage*
6. *Stepping stone path linking front and rear gardens*
7. *Stepping stone path leading to multi-stemmed feature tree*
8. *Gazebo or garden room*
9. *Lawn areas surrounded by planted borders*
10. *Existing multi-stemmed tree with seat beneath*
11. *Existing trees*
12. *New trees*

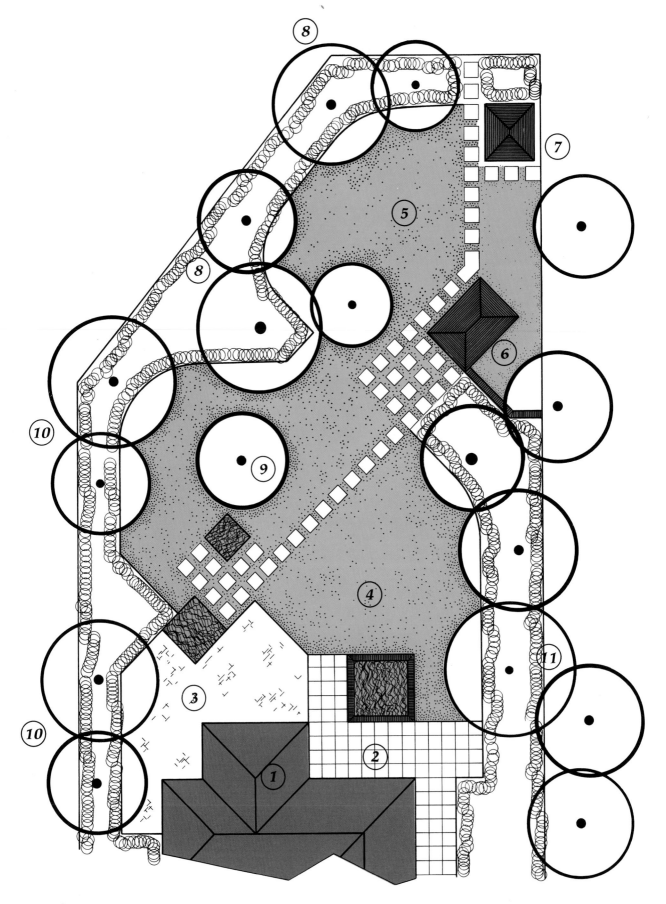

Large garden with a slightly irregular shape

On big developments builders have the freedom—within the bounds of planning requirements—to set the gardens of even large houses at a strictly limited size. However, where a smaller site is perhaps part of the extensive garden of a mature house which has been sold off to accommodate just three or four quality homes, each will have a garden that is appreciably larger than usual. This may be due to natural restrictions presented by the shape of the site or to planning requirements for minimum plot areas, for in choice semi-rural residential areas permission is often granted for a maximum density of only say three houses to an acre of land in order to maintain the generally spacious feel and degree of privacy.

Although spacious, this garden has an irregular shaped plot, the portion farthest from the house tapering quite considerably. This tends to divide the plot naturally into two parts—the regularly and irregularly shaped areas. As the garden is large anyway, the design works on the premise that it is not essential to emphasise the complete length of the garden and to work the two almost natural 'halves' into a complete, open whole—rather it goes along with the site's natural change and creates a layout which, although united and cohesive in line, makes a visual break to two sections, each perhaps of different mood and purpose.

In the part nearest to the house the emphasis is on ornamental features, with a paved area set square to the house leading to an angled patio surfaced in brick pavers or a similar material. There is plenty of scope here for overhead beams, planted pots and other forms of decoration that will soften the paving and add interest. A series of three focal points is also created by three formal ponds, the pool closest to the house featuring a bold fountain or statue, and the other two could have simple fountains set at varying heights.

A stepping stone path crosses the lawn to a gazebo or summerhouse; this together with a square 'grid' of stepping stones creates an informal area to sit, looking back towards the open lawn, the ponds and the house.

The plant borders contain a good number of trees, some of which were already established on the site, and the line of the borders extends across part of the width of the garden, cutting it visually into two. This means that the second section thus created can have a different emphasis in its use. It might have a plot for vegetables or salad crops with a greenhouse, or it might have a slightly wilder look with 'rough mown' grass and a tool shed. The grass might even feature small species bulbs and wild flowers creating the delightful feel of an old-fashioned country meadow.

Key:

1. *House*
2. *Paved area set square to house with raised feature pond*
3. *Brick paved patio set at an angle with two smaller ponds linked by stepping stones*
4. *Ornamental lawn area*
5. *Informal lawn possibly with wild flowers and naturalized bulbs*
6. *Gazebo/summerhouse with occasional sitting area to front and utility area to rear, screened by 6 ft (1.8 m) high wall*
7. *Storage shed*
8. *Group of fruit trees or small native species appropriate to 'wild' garden underplanted with suitable shrubs*
9. *Specimen tree as focal point in lawn*
10. *Existing trees*
11. *New trees in shrub border*

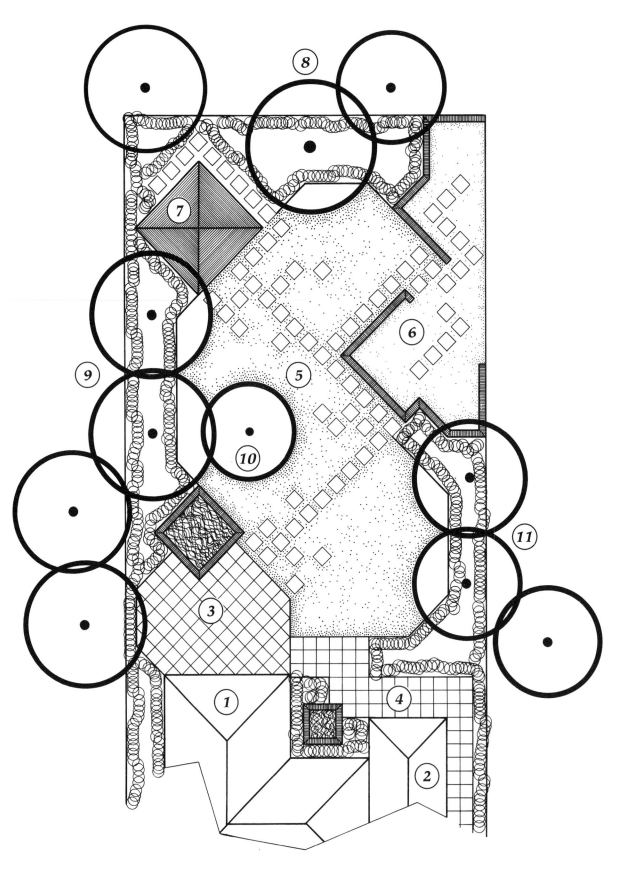

Design for a garden of substance

The design for this good sized plot is quite ambitious and intentionally so, for it is the type of layout that is appropriate to a large new house of quality and substance. All too often one sees a very attractive house—built perhaps as a one-off or in a small group of just three or four—where the materials and workmanship are obviously to a high standard and the architecture incorporates many pleasing details and finishing touches, and yet the garden is a complete let-down which does not begin to do justice to the building in its layout, its features and their construction, the materials used and even the plants. A mass of orange and yellow marigolds with red petunias can hardly be said to complement the quiet elegance of dark-stained timber garage doors set in reddish-pink rustic stock bricks.

The most irritating aspect of such a scenario—and we have observed many—is that against the house the garden looks cheap. This is almost certainly because in spite of having spent many thousands of pounds on the house itself, the purchasers are trying to do the garden on the cheap instead of acknowledging it as the vital element of the property that it indisputably is, and allocating proper funds to its development. Between five and ten per cent of the purchase price of the house would probably cover the cost of landscaping the garden, and would be capital well invested.

This design is based on squares and angles which together form a shape that is satisfying and well balanced. The main patio features angled lines and a pool with a fountain or water bubbling over pebbles; there is a further area of paving—this could be brick pavers to complement the house—which connects with the front and features a small pool or raised herb bed. The lawn is of quite generous proportion and is made more interesting by the addition of stepping stones laid in an ornamental pattern that might best be described as 'controlled random'.

There are two features of the garden which would be the most expensive to construct and would necessitate professional help but would, nevertheless, give the opportunity of echoing in the garden the architectural quality and detail of the house. Firstly there is the gazebo or summerhouse in the left hand corner, which should ideally be built using the same brick and roof tiles as the house and could consist of anything from four brick piers supporting a pitched roof to a completely enclosed garden room or summerhouse with windows and doors. Secondly, on the opposite side of the garden is a system of screening walls 6 ft (1.8 m) high, which should again echo the materials of the house and could include ornamental brickwork details. The space behind the walls can screen vegetable and fruit plots, a children's play area or just a utility and storage area.

Finally, do remember that although this garden is large and the features as described would be costly to install, the actual shape of the design could lend itself to a smaller plot of similar proportions and be adapted to incorporate, say, a simple wooden trellis instead of a wall and a pergola that is readily available in kit form instead of a one-off gazebo.

Key:

1. House
2. Garage
3. Spacious patio set at an angle with raised feature pool or plant bed
4. Wide path from patio to front of house with feature plant bed seen from kitchen
5. Lawn of geometric shape with stepping stones laid to form decorative pattern and to link the various elements of the garden
6. Produce/utility/play area screened by ornamental walls 6 ft (1.8 m) high to complement finish of house
7. Gazebo or summerhouse designed to blend with house and ornamental walls
8. New tree
9. New tree planting
10. New small weeping tree as focal point in lawn
11. Group of existing trees

The design of this fairly
large garden provides for
two separate places to sit.
In good weather, the
brick paved patio makes
a pleasant setting, but at
any time of year a path
leads beside the open,
squared lawn to an
inviting garden room
with a timber panelled
interior complemented by
light cane table and
chairs. Its huge windows
and sliding doors make it
possible to sit and enjoy
two formal pools, each
with a different fountain.
The pleasant feeling of
interest and shelter is
made complete by a
dark-stained timber
pergola.
Garden by Telford
Development
Corporation.

Design for a long, narrow, gently sloping site

A sloping site often presents householders with what appear to be enormous problems. Uncertain whether they should terrace to create a series of level areas, and if so how and where the changes in level should occur, they sometimes give up altogether and lay the garden out as though the slope did not exist. Even on a gentle slope the result can be quite unsatisfactory, for there is no flat surface on which to sit outside in comfort nor anywhere even to stand a planted pot without it needing a brick under one side!

This plot not only has a gentle fall downwards from the house; it is also rather long and narrow in shape. The fall is not so steep that you cannot walk in comfort the length of the plot, but is sufficient that if left unaltered it would be impossible to see much of the garden at all whilst sitting inside the house because everything outside would fall below eye level, cancelling out much of the pleasure that a garden can give.

So the design is planned to overcome the problems of the site in a fairly simple way by creating close to the house a level paved area that offers somewhere to sit and a view that can be enjoyed from indoors, and by introducing to the garden as a whole lines that detract from its long, narrow shape, making it feel wider and more spacious. The design could therefore be applied to a site that slopes upward or a long, narrow plot that is level. The angle of the patio not only sets the mood for this emphasis on width, but also creates a natural leading-off point for the steps dropping down approximately 18 in (45 cm) to the stepping stone path leading through the lawn to a garden room. This creates a point of interest at the far end of the garden and the opportunity to enjoy a different view by sitting and looking up towards the house, especially in cooler weather when the shelter provided by a room or summerhouse is most welcome. The curve of the borders and the almost zig-zag feel of the path again help to make the plot look wider—try covering the path on plan with a piece of paper and see how much more of a long, narrow corridor the garden appears to be.

The lawn and borders constitute the part of the garden that is quieter in mood, and the borders could be planted quite densely with shrubs as well as a number of trees, creating in time a pleasantly secluded plot. In contrast, the level patio with its free access and vision from the house is a centre of interest and activity. It is sheltered on the left hand side by a screen wall and could also feature overhead beams to create a simple pergola softened with climbing plants. The pool is another focal point, which should feature a fountain and garden lights to enliven the view even after dark. If no pool is required, this square could form the shingle or pebble covered base for a sculpture or large ornamental pot, and the patio should, in any event, be liberally decorated with planted containers creating a really pleasant ambience for a barbecue with family and friends or a quiet cup of tea on a sunny afternoon.

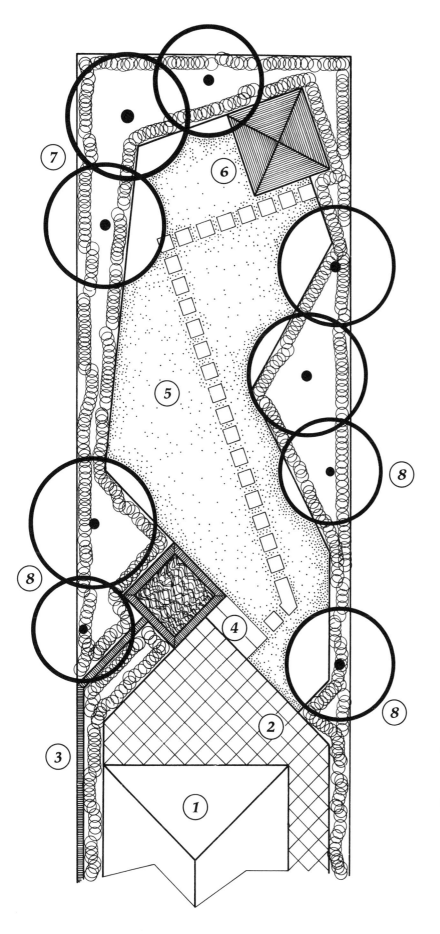

Key:

1. House
2. Patio set at angle to house with optional pergola and feature pool/plant bed
3. Screen wall 6 ft (1.8 m) high
4. Three steps leading down from patio to stepping stone path
5. Gently sloping lawn surrounded by densely planted borders
6. Garden room
7. Group of existing trees retained
8. Selection of new ornamental trees to give year-round flower and foliage interest

53

If a patio is the centre of interest in a garden design when viewed from inside the house, then there should be something appealing to see all the time — and that could mean after dark as well as in daylight.

This raised patio pool with wide surround features two sealed lamps that are safe to use underwater.

Floating on the surface, they bathe the whole area in a dramatic glow, highlighting the texture and form of plants and the soft spray of the fountain.

Even by day the area is full of interest, and yet this is a setting that is eminently achievable for many garden owners, using materials and plants readily available from garden centres.

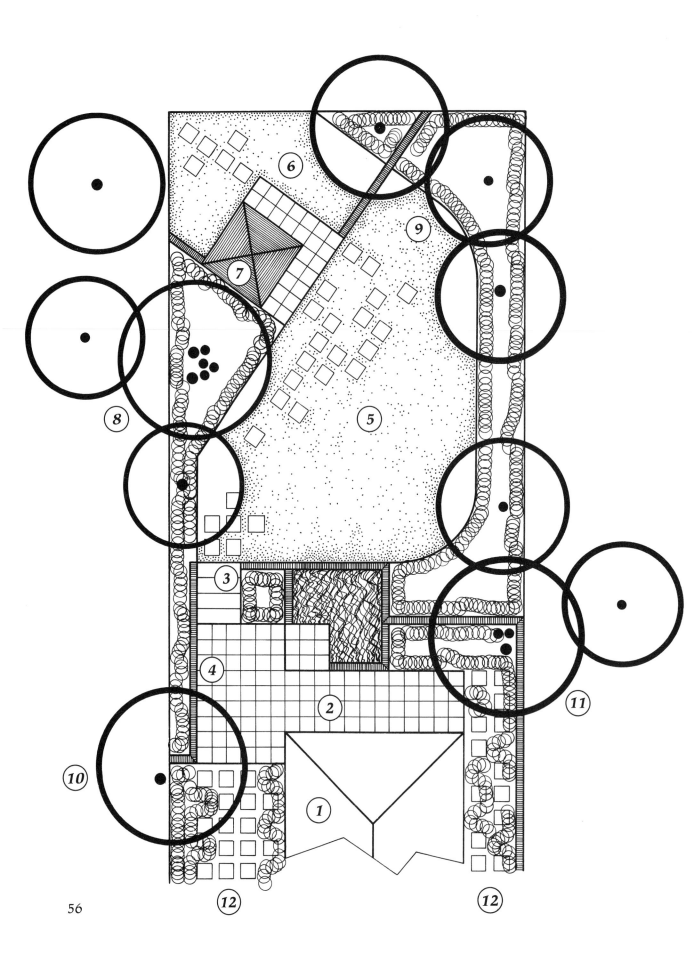

Design for a steeply sloping site

If a gently falling slope can present a problem, then a site which rises steeply away from the house can be an absolute nightmare. It is a situation that we have experienced ourselves, having once bought a new house with a garden which was so steep that the developer's sales representative actually suggested that buyers might just as well assume that they had no garden since such a site would never be usable.

Such glum and ignorant defeatism! Of course something could be done to make the garden useful and attractive. It could even be argued that developers should be aware not only of the possibilities for a sloping garden but also the extent to which householders are daunted, and should therefore landscape the site themselves, selling the house with a garden already terraced, complete with retaining walls to create level areas linked by steps. It is not unknown, for we have in the past been commissioned to do just that, designing a variation on a theme for each house in a close. Indeed, it is vital that something should be done with a garden that rises steeply from the house, not only in order to render it accessible and usable but also from a visual aspect for, unlike a falling slope, the view of a site that rises is always there, looming large every time you look out of the window.

This design is for a garden that rises by 4 ft (1.2 m) upwards from the house, and it is based on the need for the site to be split into a series of stepped areas created by the construction of retaining walls. In this case, virtually all the gradient would be taken up by this procedure, leaving only a slight slope in the central lawn.

Much of the lower level immediately outside the house is paved, creating a secluded area well sheltered by surrounding retaining walls, which should be softened with climbing plants; to either side of the house stepping stones lead through ground cover planting. This area features a large raised pool, which could be accented by a gargoyle fountain set in the wall behind, or by a central fountain or statue. It is the main focal point from the house, and the area should be decorated with planted pots and groups of pebbles arranged on the paving.

The main retaining wall includes steps which rise by 3 ft (90 cm) in total, leading to a gently sloping lawn and to a third level in the left hand corner—an area that is 9–12 in (22–30 cm) higher than the lawn. A feature of this upper level is a garden room—or summerhouse, greenhouse or shed—and the area could be used for relaxation or children's play, or for utility or vegetable and fruit plots.

The actual line of the design is worth noting. It does not rely on retaining walls in obvious straight lines across the plot, but contains contrast between the lower level, which is squared and simple in shape, and the lawn, with its regular curved border to the right giving way to a more dramatic angle on the left hand side. Not only is the summerhouse or utility screened from the house to some extent—especially by the multi-stemmed tree—but the layout also invites people to make the effort to climb the steps and see what lies at the top of the garden.

Timber features (by Ashley Cartwright for Practical Woodworking) enhance garden designs in various ways. A semi-solid screen acts as a baffle, creating privacy for a patio. The oak tree seat creates an ideal focal point for a seating area away from the house; other details here are low planting in stone chippings, wall shelves and several planted containers.

Below, black painted furniture lends an air of sophistication to the patio of a small family garden.

Design for a tapering plot

This plot is just the sort of shape that can drive people to despair and exasperation. It starts off in a fairly promising way; the left hand boundary is square with the house and straight, but then one looks across to the right hand boundary which tapers from the widest part of the plot—in this case just beyond the back of the house—to a really quite narrow rear boundary that itself goes off at a slight tangent.

The reasons for such irregularity in a site vary of course, but in this case the not uncommon cause is the fact that the house is situated on a corner plot, at a road junction, so the roads border the entire right hand boundary and dictate its shape. The main problem that people faced with this sort of site have to overcome is the decision of which line to take as a starting point for the layout and, having done so, how to fit in the remainder of the design—and also how to try to compensate for the faults of the site.

This design takes the line for the patio and central stepping stone path from the rear of the house and the left hand boundary, which is stable and fixed. It then plans the borders so that the tapering boundary to the right can be accommodated without disrupting the flow and sense of proportion.

The patio is situated to the side of the house, making use of the plot at its widest point; this means that looking from the house one would hardly notice the odd shape of the garden—only that there seems to be space for a nice roomy patio to one side. Then, as the plot starts to narrow, the design emphasises its width with two 'buttresses' in the border introducing horizontal lines.

These two areas also fulfil an important practical function, for they serve to divide the garden visually into an ornamental area near the house and a functional area at the far end—ideal for the family where the youngsters are old enough to play without the need for a constant watchful adult eye and yet need room to spread themselves, for the functional end of the lawn has ample space for a swing and climbing frame, and smaller toys can be stored in the shed or play room.

The left hand buttress is the setting for a rock feature, with boulders and pebbles set amongst shrubs and conifers—a really ornamental focal point. Indeed, all the borders could be planted fairly densely with trees and shrubs—especially the right hand side which borders the roads. Further screening for privacy and peace includes a wall to the edge of the patio and a 6 ft (1.8 m) high fence right along the boundary; for a new house, this may well be already provided by the builder.

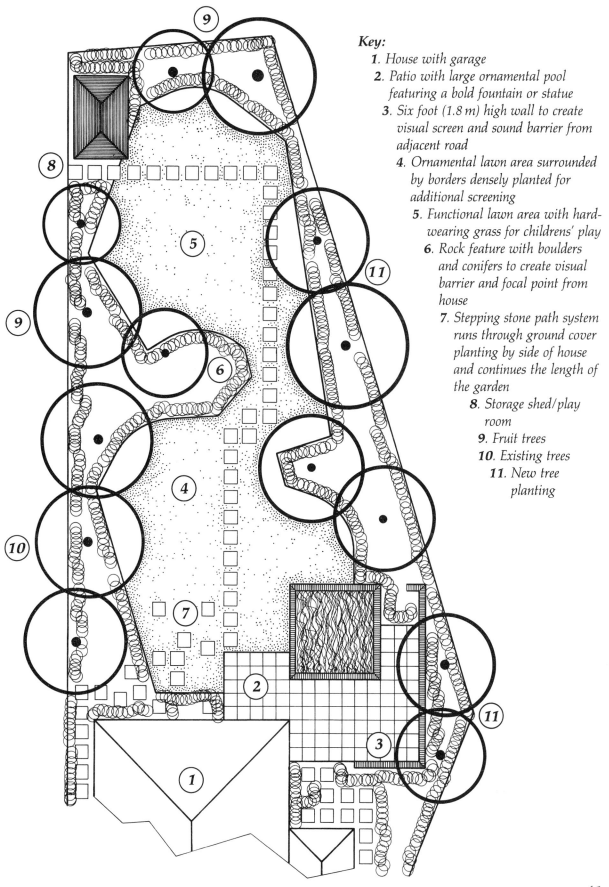

Key:

1. House with garage

2. Patio with large ornamental pool featuring a bold fountain or statue

3. Six foot (1.8 m) high wall to create visual screen and sound barrier from adjacent road

4. Ornamental lawn area surrounded by borders densely planted for additional screening

5. Functional lawn area with hard-wearing grass for childrens' play

6. Rock feature with boulders and conifers to create visual barrier and focal point from house

7. Stepping stone path system runs through ground cover planting by side of house and continues the length of the garden

8. Storage shed/play room

9. Fruit trees

10. Existing trees

11. New tree planting

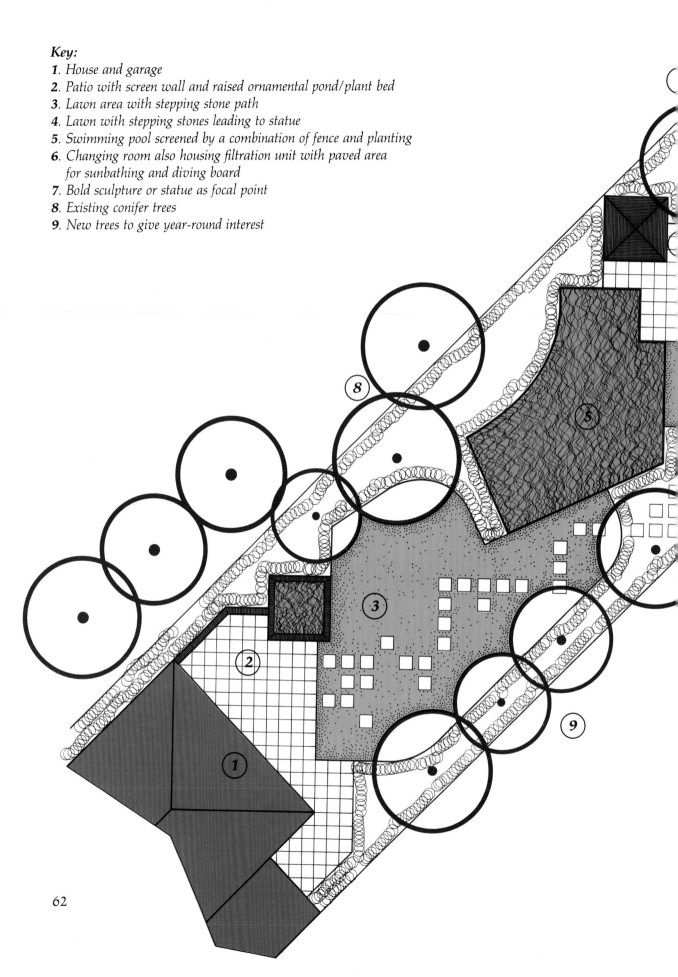

Key:

1. House and garage
2. Patio with screen wall and raised ornamental pond/plant bed
3. Lawn area with stepping stone path
4. Lawn with stepping stones leading to statue
5. Swimming pool screened by a combination of fence and planting
6. Changing room also housing filtration unit with paved area for sunbathing and diving board
7. Bold sculpture or statue as focal point
8. Existing conifer trees
9. New trees to give year-round interest

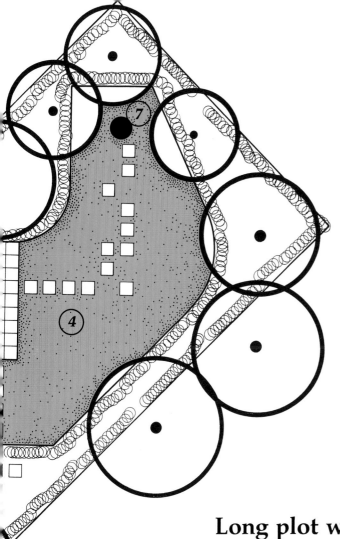

Long plot with a swimming pool

Situated in what might be described as stockbroker's belt, this garden is approximately 150 ft long and 48 ft wide (46 m × 15 m). Although quite large, its proportions are not easily suited to accommodating a swimming pool and yet such a feature would certainly be appropriate to the area and to the value of the property, enhancing its desirability. Moreover, with four teenage children in the family who bought this house—all very keen on sport—a pool was considered a priority.

Too often the mistake is made—and on a new site it is all too possible to make—of having a swimming pool installed as the first priority and then trying to plan the rest of the garden around it. The pool may then dominate the garden, the layout as a whole appearing disjointed and unco-ordinated. After all, unless it is covered the pool is probably not used for several months of the year in many climates and during those coldest months it is more pleasant to see trees, lawn, plants and ornamental features. Even in hot, sunny weather a swimming pool is much more inviting and feels more comfortable if it is screened for privacy and blends into landscaped surroundings, rather than giving the impression of an oasis in a large flat, exposed area of lawn or paving.

On a more practical note, there is also the need to house a filtration unit and any other equipment necessary for the upkeep of the pool; a changing room is desirable and safety is essential. Young children must

63

be prevented from falling into the water, especially when the pool is not in use and there is danger of them straying unseen close to its edge.

Landscaping for appearance, convenience and maximum safety are all taken into account in this design for the long, comparatively narrow garden with a swimming pool—and the pool itself is an unusual and pleasing shape. It is large enough for a family 'splash about', averaging 40 by 20 ft (12 m × 6 m) in size, and there is even space for a changing room which also houses the filtration unit.

The layout starts at the back of the house with an angled patio with screen wall and raised ornamental pool or plant bed feature. A stepping stone path leads through the lawn in a random pattern to the swimming pool area; it meanders through planting on the right hand side to a paved area where there is a diving board and steps going down into the water and where seats and a table are positioned. The path then continues through a second lawn area surrounded by curved borders with plenty of

trees for screening, and ends at a focal point, which should ideally take the form of a statue emphasising the ornamental character of this part of the garden.

To the front and left hand side of the swimming pool there is dense evergreen planting in order to deter small children from running into the pool. The open right hand side, at the end that is nearest to the house, can be bounded by an ornamental screen—perhaps in the form of a palisade-style fence about 30 in (76 cm) high. The path meandering through plants could also be completely screened by a fence and gates and the planting between the path and the edge of the pool should again be fairly dense evergreens for added safety.

The use of evergreen plants will help to prevent the pool water from being dirtied by falling leaves but with a pool in this sort of setting care would also need to be taken when maintaining the plant beds to prevent soil from falling into the water.

3 Features

The designs shown and described give ideas for ways in which a plot can be treated overall, for the first step in creating a new garden must be to decide on that framework—the form and shape that the layout of the garden will take. However, our designs have been devised so that they lend themselves to acting like a skeleton, and there is plenty of opportunity for individual choice and expression when it comes to putting flesh on the bones and giving the garden character.

Individual choices are essential; everyone wants something different and inevitably you may choose to take some aspects of one design and put them together with another, or to substitute certain features. Perhaps you like the shape for a particular plot but would prefer a seat to a pond or a shingled surface to a lawn; maybe you would rather have a rock feature than a plain border or decide to omit part of the paving or adapt the patio to accommodate a built-in barbecue. We know from experience that garden owners are likely to change this sort of detail and so we have tried to make allowance for plenty of options.

This is understandable, not only because each site is different, but also because people's tastes and desires differ. As we have said before, you may not know what you want from a new garden until something you see just seems to spark off an idea, and good ideas in gardens appear not only in their design, but perhaps even more notably in the little things, in the same way as eye-catching accessories and finishing touches can help to 'make' a room.

Of course, not everyone has a river at the bottom of their garden, but this boat was used by the students of Merrist Wood college as a stunning feature of their ingenious design for a riverside garden seen at the Chelsea Show.

The use of a boat moored to a jetty as a purely ornamental feature is justified in any garden setting where water exists or has been introduced. The design features foliage plants with strong shapes and forms combined with solid timber railway sleepers which, being impregnated with preservative, have a lasting quality. Perhaps the greatest appeal of the whole composition lies not only in its originality but in the mood of quiet contemplation verging on escapism — the impression that you could just slip the rope and drift away. What could offer greater contrast to the sameness of suburbia or the drabness of many urban settings?

So, this section on features sets out to help to bring the designs to life not only by giving advice and ideas on the range of materials available and the most appropriate choice but also what you can do with those materials using just a little flair and imagination. Some may be structural items that need planning and possibly some heavy work—positioning rocks or making a pergola or bridge—others are just a matter of placing a planted pot or a group of pots, perhaps together with some pebbles, in a composition that catches the eye, raising it above the obvious and commonplace.

One of the characteristics of a good artist is an instinctive sense of when to resist the temptation to draw another line or paint another brush stroke. A similar economy of style is advisable in gardens. There are many features and ideas shown here and when you see what is possible it is sometimes difficult to be selective, to avoid being carried away with enthusiasm. We have experienced this problem in creating our own gardens (as opposed to those for other people, where it is much easier to be objective!). Because we are aware of so many possible options, we have to be quite firm with ourselves in selecting the style of layout and features that we want and sticking to them.

The garden will probably be more successful if you refrain from overdoing it and from mixing too many styles. Outside as well as indoors, it can be nice to see a comfortably cluttered look, but remember that whatever goes into the garden has to be maintained and that pleasant clutter (as opposed to the lush informality of mixed planting) can suddenly seem to have turned into an unbearable mess. In the same way, a mixture of styles—like an interior that blends the very modern with a few well chosen antiques—can be striking and most successful, but if you mix too many styles in the garden you could create something approaching a miniature Disneyland.

Designers who dictate rigid lines and extreme economy of style can be an awful bore. Individualism is highly desirable as are innovation, decorative exuberance and even eccentricity. However, in our experience most people who are faced with making a new garden really welcome some suggestions, advice and guidance as long as it is constructive, practical and not too dictatorial. That is what we have endeavoured to present here, based on what seems to work best and to be popular with the majority of people who see it, and also, inevitably, based on our own particular style. It is a style that tends to rely, wherever possible, on materials that are readily available from garden centres and builders' merchants and nurseries and to use them in a way that is achievable in most ordinary back gardens (and some front gardens too).

It should also be said that not all of the features shown here are our own work; some were created by other designers and are included because we find them appealing and believe that they illustrate something useful. Even if some seem quite ambitious in the form in which they are illustrated, they often demonstrate a principle that can be applied on a much simpler level or show a standard of workmanship to which an amateur landscaper might aspire, although as in any craft, even a professional can spend a lifetime seeking perfection. You can hardly expect to achieve the equivalent in a couple of Saturday afternoons.

Nevertheless, many of these ideas succeed because they are well executed in a way that certainly can be emulated by home gardeners. It does matter that stonework should look neat and not be scarred with blobs of mortar that have oozed out of joints and been allowed to dry. It matters too that paving should have joints that at least approximate straight lines rather than a haphazard wiggle. However simple, a beautifully finished piece of work is always a joy, so if you are a disaster at DIY do consider enlisting professional help—many people find that it works well to employ somebody to do the heavier landscaping jobs like laying paving, building walls, perhaps installing rock, and then undertake for themselves the jobs they can face with greater confidence like laying a lawn, planting, and building a simple seat or barbecue.

This book is essentially one of ideas. We are not concerned here to go into great technical details of how to do all the things shown, but rather try to give practical guidance and to mention points worth considering. However, it would perhaps be useful at this stage to clarify the order in which the various aspects of creating a new garden should be approached.

Design obviously comes first, so that you know what you are working towards. Next, site preparation must be undertaken—any levelling, making up ground, clearing debris and so on. The heavier tasks of building the garden framework follow on—putting up a fence, building walls, laying a patio and path, creating a pond, play area or sand pit. Before laying a lawn and planting beds and borders the soil should be dug over, cleared of weeds and improved as necessary and, finally, pots and ornaments can be positioned and items such as garden furniture and outdoor lighting installed. We are well aware that the whole operation may take weeks, months or even—dare we say it?—years to complete, but it may help to know the logical order in which all the pieces should fit together.

Paving

Our designs all indicate a patio or paved area of some description, and give an idea of shape and position. Such a feature is likely to be a priority in a new garden, to provide a hard, clean surface instead of all that mud. Although it is a practical concept to have paving outside the back door—especially if your house features patio windows—it is worth emphasising again that it does not necessarily have to be your main outdoor living area particularly if the back of the house faces north and that part of the garden never gets any sun. Better to choose one of the designs that includes a second sitting area in another part of the garden and if necessary emphasise that feature by increasing its size.

The paving you use—its size, finish and colour—will largely determine the look and mood of the patio. Although it is nice to have something distinctive, the final appearance will be greatly enhanced if the material you choose blends and complements with the colour and texture of the materials in which the house is built.

Some pots are ornaments in their own right. They can be positioned in the garden in the same way as any other beautiful object and are especially effective complementing plants rather than containing them. The Ali-Baba pot above exudes an air of mystery, half-hidden by plants chosen for their sympathy with its shape and texture.

One large and two smaller pots often make a pleasing arrangement, and the set of strawberry pots in warm terracotta have a Mediterranean feel.

The single dark brown glazed terracotta urn is, in contrast, more sophisticated and is appealing both for its shape and smooth, shiny, reflective surface.

Brick paving can lend a pleasing, up-market look to a patio and is very versatile for it can be laid in many patterns and permutations, but it does take time to lay. Remember, too, that you should use bricks that are specially made as pavers or are specified as being suitable for paving.

Natural stone—especially York paving in random rectangular pieces—is another material that is extremely handsome and, in fact, can blend well with brick pavers. However, it is very expensive to buy and not always readily available. If the value of your house is towards the upper end of the property market and if you intend to stay there and enjoy the garden for a few years, then York stone would be worth considering as an investment, for it can only improve with age and weathering, which adds character to its subtle colouring and texture. However, for the majority of people the expense is hardly worthwhile, especially when there are so many attractive manufactured alternatives, some of which can offer a flavour of the texture and shading of real York at a very much lower price.

Nearly all paving now comes in millimetre dimensions that are a rough equivalent of traditional imperial sizes (for example a 2 by 2 ft slab is now 600 by 600 mm) and these larger slabs are good for a fairly generous area of paving in a medium to large garden. Some have a Riven finish like York, either in a single shade or a blend of colours that gives the effect of weathered stone. The buff and warm Cotswold type of shades, together with the subtler weathered blends of grey and buff look well with a house built in yellow or buff coloured bricks or stone, whilst pink, reddish and grey shades are better with red brick or greyish stone.

Slabs are also available with a finish that gives the impression of brick pavers and in smaller, rectangular or square modules. These are a good choice for a tiny garden or a small area of paving, for they are not only in an appropriate scale, but also offer the maximum interest of ground texture in a limited space. Some are even more obviously decorative, giving the impression of small cobbles in squared or circular arrangements. They make it possible to introduce really ornamental patterns that retain a good degree of subtlety.

Larger paving manufacturers with national distribution now offer quite comprehensive literature giving information on working out quantities, laying the material and so on. However, there are some basic practical points that are worth mentioning.

First, and perhaps most crucial, is that the finished level of a paved area adjacent to the house should be at least two courses of brickwork below the house damp proof course and should have a slight fall away from the house to allow for drainage. Secondly, never pave over a manhole cover for you must leave access to drains, and for safety's sake the finished level of the paving should be flush with the cover. It can either be disguised by a planted container—or group of containers—or replaced with a recessed cover—a metal frame into which paving slabs can be set. When in place it is detectable only by a metal outer rim and small holes into which hooks can be inserted for lifting.

Many of our designs include patios that are set at an angle to the house, and this means that some paving slabs against the house wall will need to be cut. The type of slabs mentioned here can normally be cut using a masonry hammer and bolster chisel without too much trouble (the manufacturer's literature will give details) but beware of choosing paving with a tiny pebble ('exposed aggregate') finish for this purpose because the slabs will have to be cut with an electric power tool with a carborundum disc attachment.

Decorating a paved area

However subtle the appearance of the material that you use, unrelieved wall-to-wall paving is in our opinion unpleasant, hard and unacceptable in any garden. It is also unnecessary, for there are so many ways—often quite simple—in which a patio or paved area can be softened and decorated so that it becomes a really ornamental feature of the garden, full of interest and character.

We have mentioned cutting in slabs against the house when the patio is set at an angle. This may also be necessary to create a straight edge along the boundary furthest from the house. However, an alternative is to leave a staggered edge to the paving merging it into lawn, shingle or pebbles. This will create a softer, more interesting line and the stagger could be even more varied by the addition of an occasional extra slab. The result will be a line that appears quite attractively random but actually serves a deliberately decorative purpose.

In strategic positions that are not on the main pedestrian routes across the paving it is a good idea to leave out a slab or a small, random shaped group of slabs and in their place to spread shingle, stone chippings or pebbles as a softer contrast in ground texture. All these materials are now available from garden centres in pre-packs making them convenient to use; they also come in several shades, so that you can choose one which blends or contrasts pleasantly with the paving.

Another idea for these areas of relief is to use just one or two pieces of rock, chosen for their shape and character, and positioned so that they almost take on the quality of a piece of sculpture. Look for pieces of roughly 2 ft by 1 ft (60 cm × 30 cm) in overall size for a medium sized patio and larger for a greater expanse of paving.

You may be surprised by the range of colour and texture that can be found in the rock as well as the interesting shapes—and the effects that you can achieve. Rocks positioned vertically can look quite dramatic, whilst lying horizontally they take on a pleasing sense of solidity. A combination of the two lends a hint of oriental style and the rocks can be surrounded by smaller stone chippings.

Smooth, rounded pebbles have great decorative potential as texture contrast—either as a substitute for paving in the same way as rock, or positioned on the paving itself in random groups. The secret, as the illustrations show, is to use pebbles with a slight variation in size and to position them carefully so that they appear to have 'happened' in a natural, casual manner—piled irregularly on top of each other and spil-

More pots and sculpture decorating paving and blending well with plants.

David Norris's water gatherer becomes a poolside focal point of Peter Rogers' design above, and is made even more effective by bold foliage shapes and textures.

The small glazed earthenware Chinese pot with saucer (right) is chosen to blend in colour, shape and scale with the quartered Set pavers on which it stands. Fresh green and white variegated ivy grows both in the pot and beside the paving and the theme is echoed in a group of simple white geraniums. A complete composition in a very small space.

Dark brown glazed urn with pebbles in a quite dramatic setting framed by the thrusting, sword-like leaves of Phormium tenax — excellent plants for a sheltered patio with their variety of green and red shades with distinct-ive striped variegation.

ling out individually at the edge of the group. The best combinations seem to be achieved either by the bold sweep of a confident first attempt or by a great deal of trial and error!

Although rock and pebbles have a natural sculptural quality, you may prefer to include a more formal, man-made sculpture as a focal point of the patio, and here the possibilities are obviously open to endless interpretation, according to taste and budget. Some of the widely available, mass-produced garden ornaments are singularly uninspiring but others have real possibilities, especially small classical figures and those inspired by oriental art—a Buddha or a Japanese snow lantern, for instance. Such a piece is most effective when positioned purposefully to create a real focal point; not necessarily in the centre of the patio but perhaps where it can be seen from the sitting room window or only as you step out on to the patio—even in a position of mystery, where the casual observer suddenly comes across it half hidden by planting.

It will, too, be most successful if it is positioned as if you expect it to be a dramatic high point of the scene, rather than just some object that happens to be sitting there, to one side of the patio. If you hide it from view with a table and chairs or store the wheelbarrow beside it, people will have the impression that it is not meant to be noticed, and hardly intended to take their breath away.

The type of sculpture and ornaments mentioned are obviously by no means the only choice. Antique and bric-a-brac shops can be fruitful hunting grounds for less likely objects to decorate the patio, whether in wood, metal or ceramics. An especially appealing object that will not withstand frost is nevertheless worth taking outdoors for the summer and back indoors for the winter. Natural objects like driftwood or fossils can be interesting and full of character; old chimney pots have possibilities and even gnomes need not be scorned—great for those with tongue in cheek or a penchant for endless puns of the 'gnome sweet gnome' variety!

Pots of all materials, shapes and sizes have great potential as patio ornaments—with or without plants. Singly or in groups they can either act simply as containers for plants which introduce living colour and that essential softening effect or can take on the quality of an ornamental object in their own right.

Unglazed terracotta has the nice naturally warm colour and texture of baked clay and blends readily with many backgrounds, especially of course with brick. Ornately designed Spanish and French pots and urns with a lot of detail in their shape and decoration work well without plants, as do strawberry pots. If you do choose to plant these, some herbs or ivy look just as good as strawberries and the ivy can be trimmed with scissors if it gets a bit too rampant; a variety with small, variegated leaves looks most effective.

Plain clay flower pots in medium to large sizes are inexpensive, readily available and extremely useful for a wide range of plants; half-pots too are a good choice if you want to display comparatively low-growing plants like pot geraniums or those that need the freedom to lean and cascade over the rim, like fuchsias. They seem to spread themselves more comfortably in half-pots and the overall effect is in scale, the pot and plants balancing each other and looking comfortable together. Try being extravagant with small clay flower pots and half-pots, grouping as many as twenty or so together to create a richly flamboyant mixture of plants of varying heights and colours; the result should be an eye-catching feature with a Mediterranean feel.

Glazed terracotta urns fall very much into the 'ornaments in their own right' category; the smooth, rounded shape and glossy, reflective surface make them satisfying objects to look at, and they can be useful to blend or contrast in colour themes, being available in rich dark brown, royal blue or sage green. However, they do suffer particularly from the problem that can be a drawback with any terracotta—susceptibility to frost damage. The glazed pots should be taken indoors or into a conservatory for the winter as a matter of routine. This can actually be quite useful, for they make rather distinguished additions to a sitting room or hallway, where they could be pressed into service as an umbrella or walking stick holder!

Glazed earthenware pots that are resistant to many degrees of frost—as much as 40 degrees it is claimed—are now quite widely stocked by garden centres. Made in China to traditional designs that have remained virtually unchanged for centuries, they come in earthy combinations of browns, yellows and greens decorated with dragons, birds, butterflies and flowers or in a stippled rich blue 'sky after rain' glaze. These pots are capable of making a really stunning focal point, with or without plants; the smaller designs look well in groups of three and the larger pots and urns are sufficiently dramatic to warrant pride of place on the patio.

Square wooden Versailles tubs are rather more formal in style, but wood again is a natural material that, even when stained, blends happily with plants. It also allows for versatility in that wooden planters and troughs can be fitted with castors to enable them to be moved around as needed, gracing the patio in a prominent place that can be viewed from indoors whilst plants are at their best, and wheeled quietly away for treatment or a change of plants at the end of the season.

Indeed, ringing the changes as plants in containers reach their peak and fade is a useful principle in general. Hostas, for instance, make superb patio plants between May and September, with their mass of lush foliage and their summer flower spikes, but in winter when there is nothing to see they could be taken to a less obtrusive corner of the garden.

This mobility of plants in pots means that when you come to move house again some or all of those that have become established can be taken with you. However, do remember to make it clear to prospective buyers which plants are being taken and which are to stay and to have the general principle of the arrangement written into the contract.

The range of plants that can be grown in containers is much wider than the rather commonly seen specimen conifers or flowering annuals. A small weeping tree, as well as being graceful, introduces height that is often greatly needed in a new garden; pines and conifers with striking shape or growth habit are highly ornamental, as is the corkscrew hazel,

Designer Preben Jakobsen
conceived this garden not
only as a setting for
individual pieces of
sculpture, but as a
complete sculpture in
itself with attention to
line, form and colour in
all its details. The style
of the actual pieces
ranges from starkly
abstract to elegantly
representative — both
equally emotive.
The settings too are
interesting — in an open
area of paving, to one
side of a top step and on
a brick plinth beside a
plant bed featuring the
globe lamp — yet another
sculpture?

Corylus avellana 'Contorta', with its twisted branches. The spiky foliage and architectural shape of phormiums and cordyline are striking and evergreens like rhododendron can be underplanted with small bulbs. Height can also be introduced by standard specimens of roses, fuchsias and geraniums and do not forget that a small fruit tree can flourish in a container, as can tomatoes, peppers, aubergines and herbs.

On the subject of plants to soften paving, it is worth returning for a moment to those areas of contrast at ground level, for spaces created by leaving out slabs can, of course, be filled with ground cover planting like ivy or periwinkle—both nice with miniature species bulbs growing through the foliage—or scented plants like thyme, low growing lavender or miniature ground cover roses. They can be allowed to form a mass or combined with the rock, pebbles or stone chippings already mentioned.

Similarly, climbing plants have an important role to play in decorating a patio, for they can be planted to grow against the house or against a screen, wall or fence—indeed, they are essential to soften such a feature. They can, too, help to introduce that much-needed height, for that can do a lot to create a sense of shelter and privacy in a new garden which feels open, empty and exposed.

One good way of achieving this is by planting climbers to grow up a pergola or a simple arrangement of overhead beams as a feature of the paved area—good not only in the back garden but also close to the front door if this area seems too plain. Pergolas have become quite popular in recent years and certainly have an important human, decorative and functional role in the garden, for the system of uprights and cross beams creates interest above eye level, helps to blend the house with the garden by introducing an architectural quality, shelters the patio visually—especially when clothed with climbing plants—making a pleasant, comfortable atmosphere and casts cool, dappled shade and ground shadows that can be rather appealing.

Pergolas are available in kit form which is quite versatile, offering a range of sizes and some flexibility in shape. As mentioned, if you have no space for a full-scale pergola or if you just want to echo its effect elsewhere in the garden with a hint of overhead beams, then you could use 3 in (7.5 cm) square fence posts to make a very basic combination of vertical supports and horizontal beams, perhaps sawing the edges into wedge shapes to make them more decorative and even picking out the ends with a hint of colour—red or green perhaps—to give them a visual lift.

At the other end of the scale, a more ambitious feature related to the pergola is a patio roof—an area that is enclosed either just overhead or possibly with side screens that can be left open or closed to create a complete 'outdoor room' for sitting or working. The most practical material to form the roof and side screens is corrugated plastic sheeting; although it is not very elegant in appearance it is extremely functional, being waterproof yet lightweight and translucent to varying degrees, depending on the shade you select. If used as a roof the edges and gutters can be disguised by timber facia boards, giving a more pleasing finish to the feature.

Timber also has its uses at ground level in a paved area to add interest and decoration—in the form of a bridge. This might span a patio pool, but it need not necessarily cross water for it can look equally effective linking two areas of paving that are divided by a different ground texture, whether that is low planting or—ideally perhaps—shingle and pebbles to create the impression of a dry stream bed. The bridge could be as decorative as the oriental style feature illustrated, which was designed for us by Ashley Cartwright or it could be the ultimate in simplicity—four or five fence posts stained dark brown and pinned to a cross-piece.

Plant boxes and raised pools

We have already explained that the square features which form an intrinsic part of the patio layout in the Designs section are open to personal choice and interpretation. They are indicated mostly as patio pools, and water can indeed make an appealing decorative contribution to the garden, especially close to the house. However, since very young children can suffer fatal accidents in what seems a small depth of water, we recommend that if children under, say, seven regularly use the garden then you should go for one of the many 'dry' alternatives described here, or for a bubble fountain over pebbles.

The built-in features indicated in the designs are all square, they all help to balance the shape of the garden layout, they can be either raised

Water is a valuable element of a garden, bringing a sense of soothing calm and contemplation and an attractively reflective surface. When fish are added the effect can be quite mesmerising — especially true of superbly coloured and patterned Koi carp.

A water chute is formed by timber railway sleepers and a simple pond edged with brick is set in Octavian paving.

or set at ground level, and they create a focal point to be seen from inside the house—both upstairs and downstairs—from the patio itself and looking back towards the house from the rest of the garden.

At ground level the feature can have either paving as a border or, preferably, something that denotes it more distinctly like a timber edging or bricks laid on edge. Within the square thus denoted the ground surface could be shingle with an ornamental pot or sculpture as a centrepiece, possibly raised on a small plinth of paving or brick; it could be planted with a specimen conifer surrounded by stone chippings and one or two pieces of rock; it could have a small specimen tree (possibly weeping) underplanted with bulbs—snowdrops, grape hyacinth, cyclamen, crocus—and finished with bark chippings for a rich brown colour contrast. Alternatively, the planting could be massed roses, herbs, or white geraniums, or a stunning specimen plant growing in a pot could be displayed.

If you choose to have the feature raised to a height of 12 in (30 cm) or 18 in (45 cm), then it can take the form of a brick-built or ornamental stone box finished with bricks laid on edge or wide coping stones. Backfilled with soil, it could become a plant box containing shrub roses, rhododendrons or a beautiful acer (Japanese maple). You could even create a landscape in miniature with a slow growing conifer and heathers or alpine plants combined with pieces of rock and stone chippings.

The raised box need not be open; backfilled with hardcore and paved

84

over it could make an imposing platform for planted pots or ornaments—even bonsai trees if they appeal to you. It could, too, be decorated with round pebbles and can also serve as occasional seating with scatter cushions taken into the garden.

Perhaps more welcoming as a seat or lounger is a box finished with slatted timber (set diagonally, it looks more interesting). The deck thus created is a good setting for ethnic accessories—rush mats or an Indian dhurrie, a paper parasol set casually to one side and a wicker basket of fruit. All these are obviously only temporary introductions for sunny days but can help to add a touch of style if you are entertaining outdoors.

If you do decide on a pond, then this can be made either at ground level, or raised. Moving water is always fascinating and lively, and various fountain effects can be achieved using a basic low voltage submersible pump with appropriate attachment. You might choose to have a simple, single jet of water, a solid dome of water just about 12 in (30 cm) high or a group of three smaller water 'domes'. These are useful where the pool is in a confined space or exposed to a cross breeze, for the water is not as inclined to be blown over innocent bystanders (or sitters) as it is with a taller jet.

Again, do not neglect the decorative finishing touches; the pond should be finished with aquatic plants and could contain a small number of fish; pots and pebbles can be placed on the paved surround and you might find some decorative object to float on the surface of the water. At Chelsea we have often caused quite a stir amongst visitors by decorating a pond with hollow plastic pebbles which look convincingly like real stone, yet float gently across the surface of the water blown by the breeze. The appeal, it seems, lies in turning our expectations of natural elements on their head!

Boundaries

The most basic type of boundary fence that you are likely to find in a new garden is either 'post and wire'—literally upright posts supporting a series of horizontal strands of wire—or chain link with plastic or wire mesh. Neither is particularly attractive, nor do they afford any privacy—rather they fulfil the simple purpose of denoting the boundary. (Incidentally, if you are in any doubt as to ownership and responsibility for boundaries, if the posts are on your side and the wire or mesh attached to your neighbour's side of the fence, then that boundary is yours.)

If you want to leave these existing fences but to add softening and privacy you can either use them as the background to the plant borders in the garden or plant a hedge against them (for suitable subjects see list in the Plants section) or, alternatively, plant fast growing climbers to clothe them. There are climbers listed later in the book but two fast growers worth noting are Russian vine and evergreen honeysuckle.

More privacy and shelter from wind can obviously be obtained by putting up wooden fencing panels. Available in a standard 6 ft (1.8 m) width and varying heights, fence panels come in a range of finishes. In

To be used effectively in a garden rock does not have to be built into a 'rockery'. Inspiration can be taken from the Oriental approach, using pieces of rock as an ornamental feature with plants, shingle or paving. These illustrations demonstrate authentic Chinese and Japanese styles, each of which can be a source of that inspiration. . . .

Water-worn rock at Yi-Yuan (Garden of Joy), Suzhou, China.
Chinese garden designers traditionally sought strong character in the appearance of the rocks they used, considering their craggy surface and outline, their hollows and scoops and their colour and texture. The tortuous rugged contours and

abundance of hollows in this single dramatic rock perhaps seem disturbing to Western eyes but they again emphasise the evocative qualities of rock and the contribution that it can make to the fabric of a garden as a natural element that needs no improvement, only careful and thoughtful placing.

86

Southern garden of the Hojo in the Tofukuji Temple, Kyoto, Japan. These groups of rocks in sand are intended not only to be decorative but to have a meaning. They express the Zen philosophy that by looking at nature's simplest elements a person can experience deep spiritual awakening. Dry stone gardens may be austere but are endlessly fascinating; the rocks are composed to create the effect of harmony and stability. As for their deeper more symbolic meaning, to most Western observers this will surely remain a purely personal interpretation for it would require much study to understand the nuances of the various types and periods of Japanese gardens.

our opinion the most attractive is vertical boarding, which gives an effect similar to that of close-board fencing, but this does have a 'good' and 'bad' side. To suit positions where a good face is needed on both sides of the fence, there is now a 'double-sided' panel, which combines horizontal and vertical boarding to give the same effect on both sides.

There is no need to be put off by the colour of fence panels, which is sometimes a bit too vivid—a rather fierce orangey brown finish—as they can easily be stained in a more subtle and more interesting shade. This is also a good idea when a short run of timber fencing is provided by the builder and you want to extend it—but in a slightly different timber fencing. The two will blend more happily if you stain the entire run. Creosote can be harmful to plants, but many DIY stores sell water-based stains and you could choose dark brown or a blackish shade that gives a sophisticated look or perhaps green for a more cheerful finish. The stain will give only a light shading that allows the natural grain of the wood to show through, and if you have a pergola or have used posts to make a simple bridge, then that can be stained in the same shade to give a distinctive, co-ordinated look, although you may have to vary the number of coats to get the same finish depending on the original colour of the timber.

Fencing can be used not only as a boundary, but also to create a screen or decorative feature within the garden layout. Squared trellis panels can look effective, especially if stained dark brown or painted white and clothed with climbers; roses are perhaps most traditional and combine well with clematis. Any dark stained timber, whatever its purpose, will be lifted in appearance if combined with climbers with silver or gold variegated foliage—ivies are good—or plants with white or yellow

flowers. Again climbing roses are delightful, but the yellow flowered annual canary creeper is also a good choice, as is white flowered *Clematis montana*.

Walls

A brick or stone wall is a most handsome boundary feature, offering not only privacy but also screening from sound and creating a sense of solidity and permanence.

The cost of a high wall can often be a deterrent, for it is expensive to construct in terms of time as well as materials. However, if it is well built and benefits the garden in terms of privacy and appearance, then it should prove to be a wise investment. A wall can extend the feel of the house into the garden, making the property as a whole seem somehow complete and endowing it with a sense of impressive dignity.

An existing wall will almost certainly be built in the same material as the house and should therefore be continued in the same way. If no wall exists, then you obviously have a wider choice of materials and could take as a guide either the house bricks or the paving that is used for the patio, so that all materials blend and harmonise even if they do not have an identical finish.

There is an enormous range of bricks on the market and also a good choice of manufactured ornamental walling blocks available from garden and DIY centres. They create the effect of natural stone with varying degrees of success and one block even enables you to build with a finish that looks like brick walling in a choice of two shades. The large blocks enable you to lay several 'bricks' at once, making the job easier and faster.

Normally a boundary wall—or a feature wall within the plot such as those indicated in the designs to screen vegetable plots and utility areas—will be 6 ft (1.8 m) or 6 ft 6 in (2 m) high and 9 in (22 cm) wide, consisting of a double 'skin' or thickness of brick. In many areas you will need planning permission from the local authority to build walls more than 6 ft 6 in (2 m) high within the plot and more than 3 ft (1 m) high to the front boundary, so if you want to go to a greater height it is wise to check with the planning office. Do not forget, too, that if you have an 'open plan' restriction on the front garden you should abide by its stipulation as to the height of walls, if indeed they are permitted at all.

Bearing these restraints in mind, a high wall as a feature of the garden can become a really interesting and ornamental focal point. For instance the line of the top of the wall can be varied—curved over or slightly turned up at the edge, especially if it steps down in a series of changes in level.

You might build into the wall a wrought iron panel or set in a gate, either fulfilling a functional or a purely ornamental role. Alternatively, you could build into the wall a decorative mask or even a group of masks like the eye-catching collection that we displayed at Chelsea one year, depicting heads of 'grotesques' suffering from various ailments and decorated with herbs that can cure those ailments. A simpler feature is to set

Douglas Knight has a way with rock. Here he has created an artificial setting that looks for all the world like a natural mountain stream. Westmorland slate is used in a range of sizes from massive slabs to small chippings, forming a series of waterfalls varying in depth and force. The line of the stream meanders gently and rocks are set well into the banks at an angle that suggests power and strength — strength that is contrasted by delicate waterside planting.

into the wall horizontally a series of paving slabs so that they protrude just enough to form a shelf for plants in pots or a small statue.

Lower walls are not such a massive structural undertaking and can be worthwhile features of the garden either within the site or to the front boundary if there is no restriction against this. Of course, if both sides of the wall are to be seen it needs to have a double face and to make the job easier you could use a walling block that is slightly wider than usual and has a good 'face' on either side, making it possible to build a single skin or block's width—obviously a faster and easier process.

When used for walls up to about 3 ft (90 cm) high, it can also be built with 'dry' joints, giving the effect of natural drystone walling. The blocks are simply kept in place by a small dab of mortar in the centre of each one, but there is no need to point the joints. If this process is used to build a low retaining wall against a bank of soil, then it is a good idea to make a wall garden. Soil behind the crevices will provide a home for suitable plants which will in time tumble down the surface of the blocks, merging and softening in an appealing informal way. Suitable plants include arabis, aubrieta, wallflower, pinks, rock rose, lavender, catmint, cotton lavender and edelweiss.

On a practical note, it is worth pointing out a few basic requirements for a retaining wall. It should be built to a sound foundation and as it ascends should slope slightly backwards into the bank—say 1 in in 1 ft (2.5 cm in 30 cm)—to avoid possible pressure. If the joints are mortared, then weepholes should be created close to the base of the wall to allow for drainage. Make them at about 6 ft (1.8 m) intervals by raking the mortar right out of a perpendicular joint.

Open areas

There is one feature not yet mentioned which takes up a large amount of space in most of the garden designs—an open area of lawn. When making a garden from scratch, a lawn laid from turf has advantages that are more than practical, for it also seems to give a psychological boost by creating an instantly green environment which can compensate for the time it takes for plants to mature and become established.

For these and reasons of convenience, most people find turf easy to use and quick to establish for a new lawn. Unless it is the finest quality, most turf is likely to contain some weed, but in a new garden the priority is not so much to achieve the finish of a bowling green as to get a nice covering of fresh green as quickly as possible so that the children can get outside and play and you no longer have to look at all that mud or dust!

The outline of the lawn makes a vital contribution to the shape of many of our designs and an open, level area helps to create a feeling of spaciousness. We prefer to see a lawn unbroken by plant beds, but the stepping stone paths set in grass are used in the plans as a distinctive design device. Set them slightly below the finished level of the lawn so that the grass can be cut with a hover type of mower; although they may involve a little extra effort, the stepping stones make a pleasing ground pattern in a simple way as well as fulfilling a functional purpose.

There are other ways of making a lawn more decorative and perhaps more interesting. In a strategic position it could feature a small specimen tree or conifer or a small group of trees. In the front garden especially the house could look more appealing and well-cared-for if the view is softened by, say, a weeping tree set in the lawn at a sensible distance from the house (see Plants section on trees). You could, too, plant bulbs, allowing them to naturalise in informal drifts and clumps and to flower through the grass each year. Varieties and species types of bulbs that have simpler, less showy flowers are best—narcissus, crocus, snowdrops, grape hyacinth—and a front lawn is perhaps the most practical place for them as it is likely to be walked on a good deal less than the back garden would be.

Although a lawn is traditional, close-mown grass is not essential. With the loss of so many wild flowers from the fields and hedgerows and the current justified concern for conservation, the concept of a wild flower meadow in the garden can seem very appealing. It can be difficult to establish wild flowers in existing grass, but making a lawn from scratch is the ideal situation, for you can sow a prepared mixture of seeds of grass and various flowers appropriate to your type of soil and situation and establish the two together. Mixtures are available from wild flower seed specialists and can even be made up to order; you could devote part of the lawn to this type of feature leaving another area more traditionally close-mown. 'Rough mown' grass will normally grow to 9–12 in (22–30 cm) high and can be cut once or twice a year with the blades on the mower adjusted to leave the grass as long as possible, depending on the type of flowers included. You can also make mown paths through the grass for access.

Rock features

A rock feature can make a stunning focal point on a level or sloping site, whether you choose to show off the rocks themselves with shrubs that are easy to care for, or to make them the habitat for a collection of alpine plants with their range of foliage texture and brilliant, tiny flowers. In either case it is the arrangement and positioning of the rocks themselves that will dictate whether you achieve an impressive feature or the proverbial dog's grave!

The natural formation of rocks in the landscape should be the guide to positioning rock in the garden which means that the actual pieces of rock should vary in size from good large, bold chunks which form the backbone of the feature, to smaller pieces and chippings which create 'outcrops' and help to blend the feature into its surroundings in a gradual manner. The strata of rock can usually be seen on its face; this follows the horizontal line of the earth's surface and should continue to form that horizontal line when positioned in the garden; the rocks will also look more natural if they are partially buried and on a sloping site they should tilt slightly backwards into the bank.

Above: A deceptively simple low wooden seat designed by Ashley Cartwright to echo the lines of the natural grain of timber — a device representative of his style. The warm finish of the wood is complemented by a 'scattered' arrangement of Cheshire pink pebbles to blend with foliage and flower shades.

Right: Garden furniture in light-weight wrought aluminium can be rather stark in its usual white finish, but a few cans of car spray paint effect an instant transformation to almost any shade of your choice!

This inviting setting for outdoor living features a patio roof with re-movable side screens and folding workbench with storage shelves. High-lights of the small raised brick-built pool are a domed fountain and the twisted branches of corkscrew hazel. The slatted timber seats and tables have clean, modern lines and interesting detail.

Garden design by Geoff and Faith Whiten. Roof and furniture by Practical Householder magazine.

Rock with water has immense appeal and if you want a fairly ambitious feature that makes a real talking point, then—as the illustrations show—a tumbling mountain stream combines an almost delicate charm with a sense of power and drama. However, it is not essential to go to such lengths, for by applying the same principles which succeed so well it is possible to create just a couple of rock outcrops with specimen conifers set into the lawn in a front garden or an arrangement of rocks close to the front door, making the entrance more decorative and inviting.

Garden lighting

Outdoor lighting has great possibilities in the garden and is, we believe, sadly under-used. Gentle illumination can bring a magical quality to plants and features that are quite pedestrian in the cold light of day; it also enables you to be selective, highlighting only the most desirable features of your garden, and extends the hours during which you can enjoy looking at them. This can be especially encouraging if you work hard on the garden at weekends and then hardly see it at all during the week because you are out all day.

You could, of course, have high-powered lights installed by an electrical socket and a cable runs to a transformer, which converts the surprisingly easy and, if arranged with care, can be impressively effective. The package available from garden centres works on a basic principle with the emphasis on safety. The system plugs into an ordinary indoor electrical socket and cable runs to a transformer, which converts the power to a very low voltage. From here, a weatherproof cable leads into the garden and lamps can be attached to it at any point; they can be spiked into the ground or fixed to a wall, fence or tree.

Two designs are most widely available. One looks rather like car headlamps and is very good for spotlighting or casting a coloured glow (there are four interchangeable colour filters) although it is not especially ornamental in itself. The second is a nice looking mushroom-shaped design that in open areas is acceptable as a daytime ornament, as well as casting a soft, diffused glow after dark.

A spotlight effect can be used either to illuminate a plant or object from behind—its outline will be silhouetted—or from the front, when details of its texture or foliage will be highlighted. You might conceal a lamp amongst planting beside the patio, using either blue and green light to give planting a cool, mysterious glow or red and yellow to cast a warm feel over brickwork, a clay pot with red geraniums or a sculpture. Lighting fixed to the top of a pergola and disguised by a climber can illuminate a romantic place to sit.

Lights are for safety and security as well as for decoration; use them to illuminate steps or the front entrance to the house. They are also quite magical when combined with water—below a fountain, across the water surface; try blue and green to highlight slabs of grey rock with water tumbling over them. Sealed lamps for use underwater are also available, so that the pool can be lit from inside although again the best effect is achieved by a combination of no more than two colours.

For the best effects it is necessary, too, to balance the intensity of light indoors and out. You will want to be able to sit in the house and admire the illuminated features of the garden, but if the light in the room is too strong, you will see only reflections in the window.

Garden furniture

Our garden designs without exception include spacious paved areas which are intended to be used as an outdoor room, and therefore require some kind of garden furniture. Whilst sun loungers and deckchairs are most likely to be taken out as and when the sun shines, we do believe that a patio looks smarter and more pleasant all the year round if it is furnished with a permanent table and chairs—or possibly built-in seats or benches which are decorated with cushions when needed.

The range of garden furniture available is now extremely wide and your selection will obviously depend on your taste and budget, but it will certainly set off the garden and look smarter if its colour and finish blends with other features and materials. Remember, too, that if you are likely to want to move the furniture around from time to time—quite likely if you go for a design with more than one paved area—then weight and mobility are strong considerations.

Although it is practical and attractive to leave furniture out all the year round, it can look rather dowdy after a long winter. Obviously you can clean it up, but you might consider going a stage further and buying a new set of cushions each spring—there are many in well designed fabrics available cheaply from high street stores—to ring the changes. The colour theme can be echoed in a parasol for the table and even in paper napkins or a tablecloth.

Furniture in lightweight wrought aluminium, which is normally sold only in a white finish, can undergo an even more dramatic facelift for in spring, when it is bound to look quite jaded and grubby, it can be sprayed an entirely new colour using spray cans of car paint. They are obtainable from car accessory shops in numerous colours so you might have smart, sophisticated black table and chairs one year and wine red or even jaunty mustard yellow the next! The main aim is to create a garden with style and individuality—a garden that is inviting and desirable. Isn't that surely what everybody wants?

4 Plants

The overall design of a garden helps to make the most of the available space, and the decorative features that are included help to give it interest and character, but the one element that—more than any other—will bring the garden to life with vital, constantly changing colour and movement is of course its planting.

As with every other aspect of the garden, there is plenty of scope for individual choice as to the range and type of plants that you want to include, depending as much on the amount of gardening that you want to do as on the overall 'look' that you prefer. However, we find that although everyone has their favourite and most disliked flowers and plants, there is a certain amount of basic information and advice that is always useful, especially when plant borders are being revised and re-shaped or formed from scratch.

This includes practical advice on how to combine plants to create an attractive overall picture and on which plants are suitable for certain soils and conditions. Most people creating a new garden are also looking for ideas—ways of using plants to achieve effects that they may not have thought of and suggestions for plants worth seeking out as they browse through catalogues or around the nursery or garden centre. This section sets out to cover all those aspects of planting in a way that lends itself to quick and easy reference.

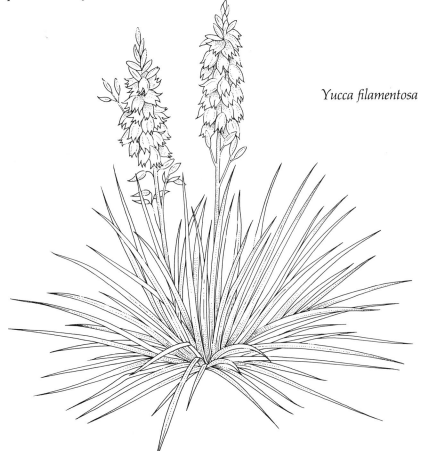

Yucca filamentosa

Opposite page
A well planned lawn with dense tree planting in the garden at Great Comp in Kent. The effect is to create one main, long vista that is partially interrupted at intervals by planting that extends into the lawn area, giving the garden an air of mystery and intrigue and inviting one to see what might lie around the next corner.

Choosing plants

Just as the decision over which house to buy is made as much with our heart as with our head—that instinctive feeling that we could develop a comfortable sense of belonging in one place and not another—so decisions over which plants to grow in the garden are primarily a matter of personal preference. However, most plant lovers find that they have to be fairly firm with themselves, for a collection of plants that are chosen at random and on sheer enthusiastic impulse does not necessarily make for the most successful garden.

It really does make sense, when looking for plants and planning what to grow where, to think of how each one will work for you, fulfilling a useful purpose as well as looking pretty, thriving in its given position and combining happily with other plants around it to create a complete picture—and not just for a few weeks of the year.

Everyone wants to look at something interesting and attractive all year round and so it pays to take as your starting point a basic framework of permanent plants—trees, shrubs and conifers, and to some extent herbaceous perennials and bulbs. These can provide an ever-changing series of high points, for flowers, foliage, stems, berries, bark or simply the outline form of the plant itself can all fascinate and delight.

A good selection of permanent plants ensures that the garden will never look bare or dull, for at any time of the year there will always be something that is at its best.

In planted borders it may seem obvious to position taller plants to the back and lower growing subjects to the front, spreading and softening the edges, but it is perhaps not quite so obvious that these two extremes usually work best if there is in some parts of the border a middle layer of plants—those that are medium growing (say 3–5 ft or 90–150 cm tall)—and in others an occasional highpoint: a plant that throws up long, narrow flower spikes perhaps, creating dramatic relief from the generally banked effect.

Plants can be made to fulfil a purpose not only in the massed effect of a border. Climbing plants, too, are extremely useful; we have mentioned their valuable role in softening stonework or timber features, but they can also be grown into a tree, against the wall of the house or even along the ground. Indeed, a mass of planting at ground level is another very useful device. Ground cover plants can soften paving, create a more interesting texture than grass in certain areas, solve the problem of what to plant on an impossible bank or under a large tree, and on a practical note can even help to suppress weeds.

The shape and form of a plant are as important as its details of leaf and flower, and it is good to have a selection of those that merge happily with others and those which are so striking and distinctive in their outline that they seem to demand pride of place in an open position. Although such plants can be grown as individual specimens, most shrubs in a border look well if planted in informal groups, usually of three or five, especially the medium to low growing subjects. It is important, too, to allow sufficient space for shrubs to grow to their optimum size; while

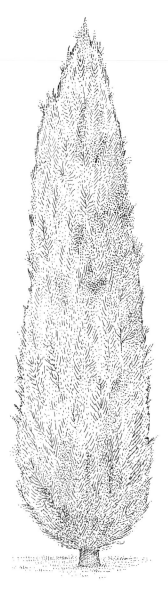

Juniperus virginiana
'Skyrocket'

Fatsia japonica

they are still young and rather small, you can use plants of a more temporary nature—annual and biennial flowers that can be grown quickly and easily from seed—to fill in any bare spaces between them. Bulb flowers, too, can fulfil this useful role.

The selections of plants listed are inevitably personal ones and the emphasis is on a range of basic plants to cover most people's needs when planting a new or replanned garden. We have been especially careful to include all those plants that we find useful and appealing for their architectural shape or their striking colour, their versatility or their frequent ability to fill spaces that seem impossible, and somehow to complete a perfect composition.

Brief practical information is given on preferred soil, position and so on but it is wise to check when buying locally on which plants do well in your area and to heed growing instructions and hints when they appear on labels and packaging. A good nurseryman's catalogue can also prove invaluable reference.

For readers in the United States plants are given a number which indicates their hardiness zone rating as determined by the Arnold Arboretum and indicated on the map at the back of the book. Please remember, however, that these ratings are only a guide; if a plant is grown in a sheltered position it may well thrive in a much colder zone and, of course, conditions can vary even within the zones indicated.

Trees

Trees are vitally important in gardens; they give a sense of height and a feeling of shelter and intimacy as well as balancing the scale of lower-growing plants. Trees cast pleasant shade; the movement of their branches is pleasing to see and the rustle of their leaves soothing to hear. The contribution that they make to our environment is essential—the more so because so many trees have been lost in recent years due to land development or disease.

We believe that developers should leave as many existing trees as possible when they build houses on a new site. When this does not happen it is perhaps a matter of conscience that we should plant new trees for the future, to replace those that were destroyed in order to build our houses. However, in planting for the future we should plant sensibly.

If a tree is planted too close to the house its branches could eventually dislodge the gutter or roof tiles, it may block out light or even break a window in high winds. The roots could disturb the foundations of the house or the drains, causing extensive damage that is costly to rectify; this is a particular problem on shrinkable clay soil where roots can penetrate amazing distances in their search for water.

It is almost impossible to specify with certainty which are 'safe' trees to plant and in what position it is 'safe' to plant them, but it certainly makes strong sense to choose a tree whose ultimate height and spread is in keeping with the size of your garden, and to plant it—as a rule of thumb—a minimum 16 ft (5 m) away from the house.

Trees can be attractive for their shape, especially a weeping specimen (which often has Pendula in the name) or an upright, feathered tree which has a single trunk but side branches emerging right down almost to ground level (and often has Fastigiata or Erecta in the name). They can offer spring or summer flowers, attractive foliage that turns fiery red in autumn and even decorative bark. A selection of these different types from our list of trees will help to ensure varied interest for many months of the year.

TREES

This lists small to medium sized garden trees that are generally available commercially. Figures give the probable height and diameter of spread after approximately twenty years in average conditions. Obviously many are likely to continue growing considerably.

Name	Comments	Height and spread
Acer ginnala	Small and spreading. Bright green leaves, fiery red in autumn.	13 × 13 ft (3.9 × 3.9 m)
griseum (paperbark maple)	Slender tree. Brilliant autumn leaves and attractive peeling bark. Suitable chalky soil.	15 × 8 ft (4.5 × 2.4 m)
negundo 'Variegatum'	Spreading, open tree. Silvery-white variegated leaves.	20 × 20 ft (6 × 6 m)

Name	Comments	Height and spread
pseudoplatanus 'Brilliantissimum'	Small, mop-headed, slow growing. Leaves brilliant pink/bronze when first open.	13 × 8 ft (3.9 × 2.4 m)
Amelanchier lamarckii	Tree or multi-stem shrub. Clouds of white flowers April. Leaves orange/red autumn.	23 × 17 ft (7 × 5 m)
Betula pendula 'Fastigiata' (feathered silver birch)	Straight upright branches. Good for small gardens.	25 × 10 ft (7.6 × 3 m)
pendula 'Youngii' (Young's weeping birch)	Lovely small tree, branches weeping right to ground.	15 × 15 ft (4.5 × 4.5 m)
Carpinus betulus 'Columnaris' (fastigiate hornbeam)	Forms a narrow column.	18 × 7 ft (5.5 × 2.1 m)
Cercis siliquastrum (the Judas tree)	Slowly grows to small tree/large rounded bush. Purple-pink flowers April–May. Large rounded leaves.	15 × 10 ft (4.5 × 3 m)
Crataegus × lavallei (May)	Upright tree, later spreading. Large white flowers May/June. Orange berries autumn–winter.	20 × 15 ft (6 × 4.5 m)
oxycantha (hawthorn)	Coccinea Plena (Paul's double scarlet) red flowers.	20 × 15 ft (6 × 4.5 m)
	Rosea Flore Pleno. Double pink flowers.	20 × 15 ft (6 × 4.5 m)

Magnolia soulangiana

103

Name	Comments	Height and spread
Gleditsia triacanthos 'Sunburst' (thornless honey locust)	Broad headed tree. Bright yellow fern-like leaves.	20 × 15 ft (6 × 4.5 m)
Laburnum vossii	Small, round-headed. Scented yellow flowers June. Seed poisonous, but this produces little.	25 × 15 ft (7.6 × 4.5 m)
Magnolia kobus	Pyramid shaped tree, spreading later. After 10 years scented cream-white flowers April.	25 × 20 ft (7.6 × 6 m)
Malus coronaria 'Charlottae'	Rounded, spreading tree. Pink scented double blossom; yellow fruits.	15 × 8 ft (4.5 × 2.4 m)
'Golden Hornet'	Upright, then broader. White flowers, bright yellow fruit.	25 × 12 ft (7.6 × 3.6 m)
'John Downie'	Upright growing, later arching. Buds pink, open to white. Bright orange–red fruit, good for jelly.	20 × 12 ft (6 × 3.6 m)
'Profusion'	Broad headed. Leaves copper–crimson then bronze–green. Purplish-red flowers, deep red fruit.	20 × 15 ft (6 × 4.5 m)
'Royalty'	Fairly upright, later spreading. Leaves deep purple; flowers pink; fruit wine–red.	15 × 10 ft (4.5 × 3 m)
sargentii	Very small, pretty tree. Scented white flowers, red currant-like fruit.	10 × 8 ft (3 × 2.4 m)
tschonoskii	Pyramid shaped. Leaves silvery when young, brilliant autumn colours. Flowers pinkish–white, rarely fruits.	30 × 8 ft (9 × 2.4 m)
Prunus cerasifera 'Nigra' (purple-leafed flowering plum)	Grey branches. Leaves open red then purplish–brown. Flowers pink March/April.	20 × 15 ft (6 × 4.5 m)
Prunus 'Accolade'	Flowering cherry with graceful spreading habit. Masses pink flowers with fringed petals April.	25 × 15 ft (7.6 × 4.5 m)
× hillieri 'Spire'	Feathered at first, later conical. Soft pink flowers April. Autumn leaf colour.	20 × 10 ft (6 × 3 m)
'Kanzan' (Sheraton cherry)	Glistening, peeling bark, rich pink double flowers.	30 × 25 ft (9 × 7.6 m)
Prunus 'Erecta' (Ama no Gawa) (Lombardy poplar cherry)	Tall, narrow, fastigate tree. Pale pink flowers April/May.	15 × 3 ft (4.5 × 1 m)
'Longipes' (Shimidsu Sakura)	Spreading, flattish crowned tree. Pink buds, large double white flowers May.	12 × 12 ft (4.5 × 4.5 m)
'Cheal's Weeping'	Good weeping shape. Double rose pink flowers April.	15 × 15 ft (4.5 × 4.5 m)
Pyrus salicifolia 'Pendula' (willow-leafed pear)	Small tree, flowing weeping branches. Leaves grey–green, white flowers April.	20 × 15 ft (6 × 4.5 m)
Robinia pseudoacacia 'Frisia'	Erect branches, round head. Bright yellow foliage.	25 × 15 ft (7.6 × 4.5 m)
pseudoacacia 'Fastigiata'	A tight column of branches with attractive green foliage.	30 × 8 ft (9 × 2.4 m)
Salix caprea 'Pendula' (Kilmarnock willow)	Small umbrella-shaped weeping tree with stiff branches.	10 × 6 ft (3 × 1.8 m)
purpurea 'Pendula' (American weeping willow)	Graceful narrow tree. Long branches tinted purple, long slender leaves.	10 × 7 ft (3 × 2 m)

Name	Comments	Height and spread
Sorbus aucuparia (rowan)	Round or oval headed tree with sharply toothed leaves. Red berries August.	25 × 15 ft (7.6 × 4.5 m)
'Embley'	Upright then spreading. Orange–red berries, autumn leaf colour.	25 × 15 ft (7.6 × 4.5 m)
hupehensis	Strong growing but compact. Bluish leaves turn red in autumn. Pale green berries turn whitish pink and last until Christmas.	25 × 15 ft (7.6 × 4.5 m)
'Joseph Rock'	Tree erect and compact. Leaves fresh green summer, copper tints in autumn. Yellow berries.	25 × 15 ft (7.6 × 4.5 m)
vilmorinii	Round, spreading head. Pretty feathery foliage turns red in autumn. Pink berries.	15 × 10 ft (4.5 × 3 m)
aria 'Lutescens' (whitebeam)	Quite tall but pyramid shape, later spreading. Leaves green upper surface, yellow down beneath in spring, greyish down in summer.	20 × 15 ft (6 × 4.5 m)

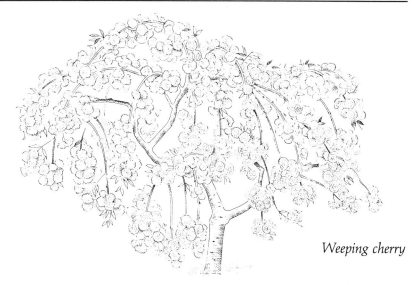

Weeping cherry

USA HARDINESS RATINGS FOR TREES LISTED

Name	Zone	Name	Zone
Acer ginnala	2	Laburnum vossii	5
Acer griseum	5	Magnolia kobus	5
Acer negundo 'Variegatum'	2	Malus (all varieties)	4
Acer pseudoplatanus 'Brilliantissimum'	5	Prunus cerasifera 'Nigra'	3
Amelanchier lamarckii	4	Prunus (other varieties)	5–6
Betula pendula	2	Pyrus salicifolia 'Pendula'	4
Carpinus betulus 'Columnaris'	4	Robinia pseudoacacia	3
Cercis siliquastrum	4	Salix caprea 'Pendula'	4
Crataegus × lavallei	4	Salix purpurea 'Pendula'	4
Crataegus oxycantha	4–6	Sorbus aucuparia	3
Gleditsia triacanthos 'Sunburst'	4	Sorbus (other varieties)	5

Shrubs

Bold, glossy dark green leaves or finely cut purple foliage can offset brickwork dramatically; light, creamy variegations contrast delightfully with dark-stained timber; a symphony of grey and silver leaved plants is cool, quiet and classy whilst golden foliage—especially that of evergreens—brightens up the garden all year round. This selection of shrubs will enable you not only to choose the right plants for the conditions in your garden but also to blend and contrast colours and textures, creating a garden of varying moods and effects. The sizes indicate the likely ultimate height of plants, which will of course vary according to conditions. They are intended as a simple, general guide for ease of planting.

Small = up to 3 ft (90 cm)
Medium = 3–6 ft (90–180 cm)
Large = 6 ft plus (180 cm plus)

Name	Comments	Size	US Hardiness Zone
Acer palmatum	'Japanese Maple'. Lovely foliage; bright autumn colour. Sheltered position; tolerant some lime but all following forms need neutral or lime-free soil.	large	5
'Atropurpureum'	Purple leaves, spreading habit.	medium–large	5
'Dissectum'	Very slow growing shapely bush. Finely cut green foliage	small, spreading	5
'Dissectum Atropurpureum'	Purple form of 'Dissectum'	small, spreading	5
Aralia elata	Handsome suckering plant; huge leaves, branched panicles white flowers Aug/Sept. Fast growing.	large	3
Arundinaria in variety	'Bamboo' makes good evergreen screen. Spreads fast; happy under trees. Most varieties large but variegata best in small spaces.	small to large in variety	5
Berberis thunbergii	A deciduous 'Barberry'. Stiff thorny branches; cream flowers in spring, red berries and foliage in autumn.	medium	4
× stenophylla	Evergreen. Forms thickets; golden scented flowers Apr/May.	large	5
verruculosa	Evergreen. Arching branches, glossy leaves, golden flowers.	medium	5
Buddleia alternifolia	Soft purple flowers June attract butterflies. Any soil.	large	5
davidii in variety	Broad, open growth. Long, sweet smelling flower panicles Jul/Aug. Colours white, red, mauve, acc to variety.	large	5
Buxus sempervirens	'Box'. Distinctive evergreen makes good specimen shrub/small tree. Slow growing. Also clipped, shaped pyramids.	large	5
Camellia japonica in variety	Choice evergreen. Lovely flowers late winter/early spring white, pink, red – many varieties. Needs lime-free soil and sheltered position; good against a wall.	medium	7
Ceanothus in variety	'Californian Lilac'. Lovely blue flowers; deciduous forms best in sunny border, evergreens best against a warm wall.	large	3
Choisya ternata	'Mexican Orange Blossom'. Bushy evergreen with glossy foliage, fragrant white flowers May.	large	8
Cordyline australis	Architectural shrub with spiky, evergreen leaves. Good in pot, where can be protected from frost.	medium	
Cornus alba 'Spaethii'	Spreading shrubs make thickets of stems. Striking red bark in winter, golden variegated leaves all summer.	medium–large	2
stolonifera 'Flaviramea'	'Yellow-stemmed dogwood', has soft green leaves.	medium–large	2
Cortaderia 'Argentea'	Tall pampas grass. Silvery plumes in autumn. Evergreen.	large	5
pumila	Dwarf form with shapely plumes on upright spikes.	small	5
Corylus avellana 'Contorta'	Form of hazel with twisted branches; yellow catkins. Feb.	large	4
Cotoneaster divaricatus	Tall, fast growing. Glossy leaves; autumn colour and berries.	large	5

Acer palmatum

Name	Comments	Size	US Hardiness Zone
microphyllus	Forms medium sized hummocks. Tiny evergreen leaves, red berries.	small, spreading	7
'Skogholm Coral Beauty'	Prostrate evergreen ground cover; large orange berries.	small, spreading	5
Cytisus praecox	'Broom'. Rounded bush, mass of cream-yellow flowers. May.	medium	5
scoparius	Numerous named hybrids with cream, yellow, bronze or crimson flowers. These dislike chalk.	medium	5
Daphne mezereum	Lovely fragrant deep red flowers. Feb/March. Thrive in open position in rich soil, cool and moist but well drained.	small	4
Deutzia × 'Mont Rose'	Easy and reliable. Large mauve-pink flowers June/July.	medium	4
Eleagnus pungens 'Maculata'	Golden variegated evergreen. Good winter foliage effect.	medium	3
Escallonia 'Donard Radiance'	Shiny leaves, pink flowers June. Ordinary soil; semi-evergreen.	medium	7
Euonymus fortunei varieties	Evergreen useful for any soil; ground cover or climbing. Some variegated, good for winter foliage colour.	small, spreading or climbing	4
Fatsia japonica	Evergreen foliage plant with superb large, leathery dark green leaves. Spreading shape. Good in town gardens.	medium	8

Name	Comments	Size	US Hardiness Zone
Forsythia × 'Lynwood'	Rich yellow flowers early spring before leaves appear. Open, branched shape, thrives in any soil.	medium–large	4
Fuchsia 'Riccartonii'	Vigorous hardy fuchsia has scarlet/purple flowers. August.	large	
'Tom Thumb'	Dwarf, compact habit. Lots of violet/carmine flowers.	small	
Garrya elliptica	Bushy, fast growing evergreen, shiny leaves, large silky pendulous catkins midwinter. Good against north or east wall.	large	
Genista lydia	Form of gorse with grey-green shoots forming hummock. Small bright yellow flowers May/June. Sunny position.	small	
Hebe anomala	'Veronica'. Rounded evergreen bush with small yellowish green leaves. White flowers in spikes. July/Sept.	medium	8–9
cupressoides	Dense evergreen rounded bush; pale blue flowers. June/July.	medium	8–9
pinguifolia 'Pagei'	Small hummocks blue/grey; white flowers. Ground cover.	small	8–9
Hydrangea	Mophead types have familiar bold flower heads, pink in limy soils, blue in lime-free soil. Lacecap types have flatter flower heads with softer, lacy appearance.	medium	6

Aralia elata

Name	Comments	Size	US Hardiness Zone
paniculata 'Grandiflora'	Broad bush with large leaves and superb tapering white flower panicles. Aug/Sept.	large	4
Hypericum androsaemum	Semi-evergreen flowers profusely June/Oct. Yellow flowers, black berries. Thrives in any soil.	small	7
calycinum	'St John's Wort'. Vigorously spreading familiar ground cover plant with large yellow flowers. Almost any soil or position.	small	5
Ilex aquifolium	Holly is slow growing but makes very useful evergreen specimen shrub or small tree on almost any well-drained soil. Good range named varieties including white and golden variegated.	medium–large	6–7
Kerria japonica	Tall, graceful, easy shrub with yellow flowers. April/May.	large	4
Lavandula spica	Old English lavender; evergreen, flowers July/Sept.	small	
'Munstead Dwarf'	Lovely dark lavender blue flowers on silvery foliage.	small	
Magnolia × soulangiana	Large shrub/small tree, wide spreading shape good as specimen in larger garden. Lovely tulip shaped flowers April/May.	large	5
stellata	Smaller, rounded shrub best for small gardens. White, scented semi-double star-shaped flowers March/April.	medium	4
Mahonia aquifolium	Evergreen with striking shiny foliage, fragrant golden flower spikes March/April. Good ground cover – spreading and low.	small	4–5
× 'Charity'	Superb architectural shrub, rosettes of large, distinctive leaves; clusters yellow flowers late January onwards. Fragrant.	medium–large	4–5
Philadelphus 'Belle Etoile'	'Mock orange blossom'. Beautifully scented single white flowers June/July on broad shrubs with semi-arching branches.	medium	5
coronarius 'Aureus'	Fresh yellow foliage, creamy white semi-double flowers.	medium	4
Phormium	'New Zealand flax'. Excellent architectural plants with sword-like leaves, rigid or arching. Varieties offer green or variegated leaves – cream, yellow or dusky pinks. Sunny position; protect crown in hard winter.	small, medium, large according to variety	
Potentilla fruticosa 'Katherine Dykes'	Potentillas are easy to grow and valuable for long flowering period. This variety – yellow flowers all summer. Sunny position.	medium	2
'Sunset'	Flowers deep orange – brick red.	small	2
Prunus laurocerasus 'Otto Luyken'	Compact form of laurel tolerant heavy shade even under trees. Spreading shape, narrow shiny green leaves.	medium	6
Rhododendron (including Azaleas)	Numerous varieties and species of this very useful evergreen shrub with showy blooms usually May/June. Good as specimens or in border ranging in size from miniature to huge, tree-like shrubs. Lime-hating; thrive in sandy soil with peat.	small–large acc. to variety	4–5

Name	Comments	Size	US Hardiness Zone
Azalea (deciduous)	Brilliant coloured flowers May/June on tough, twiggy bushes. Numerous named varieties, most fragrant.	medium–large	3
Azalea (Japanese, evergreen, semi-evergreen)	Showy low-growing plants with bushy foliage and bright flowers. Lime-free soil essential. Shelter from wind.	small	5
Rhus typhina	'Stag's Horn sumach'. Large suckering shrub/small tree with big fern-like leaves, brilliant autumn colour.	large	3
Ribes sanguineum 'Pulborough Scarlet'	Flowering currant good for quick effect. Upright stems, deep red flowers April/May.	large	5
Rose (species and shrub)	Better for all-round effect and shape than hybrid teas and floribundas. Easy to grow in sunny place, any soil. Numerous species and shrub varieties available, from very old to recent introductions so can be useful for decorative foliage, autumn heps, ground cover as well as beauty of flowers – often fragrant.	various	2–5 acc. to variety
Senecio Dunedin Hybrid 'Sunshine'	Evergreen grey foliage useful for winter colour. Low growing mounded shrub; yellow flowers summer; dry sun.	small	
Spiraea × bumalda 'Anthony Waterer'	Low twiggy shrub useful for quick effect; green leaves sometimes variegated pink/cream. Carmine flowers July/Sept.	small	4
Symphoricarpus alba	'Snowberry'. Easy shrubs, grow almost anywhere and spread by suckers. Clumps of upright shoots, milky white berries autumn/winter.	medium	3
Syringa vulgaris	Numerous named varieties of lilac available, many scented. Useful for any soil, especially chalky clay. Full sun best.	large	3
Viburnum × bodnantense	Good winter flowering viburnum; upright, fast growing. Scented flowers are frost resistant. Any reasonable soil.	large	
davidii	Autumn berrying type has deep green leaves, small white flowers June, turquoise-blue berries if planted in groups for cross pollination. Dense, low mound, spreading shape.	small	8
rhytidophyllum	Spring flowering type. Large, fast-growing rounded bush – similar effect rhododendron but good on chalk. Evergreen.	large	5
Weigela hybrida 'Newport Red'	Upright shrub has profuse red flowers June. Semi-shade in rich moist soil.	large	5
Yucca filamentosa	Architectural plants of exotic appearance with stiff, spiky leaves. Magnificent creamy white flowers on long stem above plant July/August. Evergreen; sunny position.	small	5

Climbing plants

Climbers have a great contribution to make to a garden that is being reshaped or created from scratch—probably greater than is usually acknowledged. They can do so much to clothe and soften fences, walls, pergolas, patios, sheds, screens and trellises—and many do the job at an encouragingly fast rate! They tumble as well as climb, they combine well with other plants and the range means that you can have interest of flower and foliage all year round. The ultimate size of plants will obviously depend on conditions, the amount and type of support and the way in which the climber is trained.

Left

Parthenocissus quinquefolia

Right

Lonicera Aureo-Reticulata

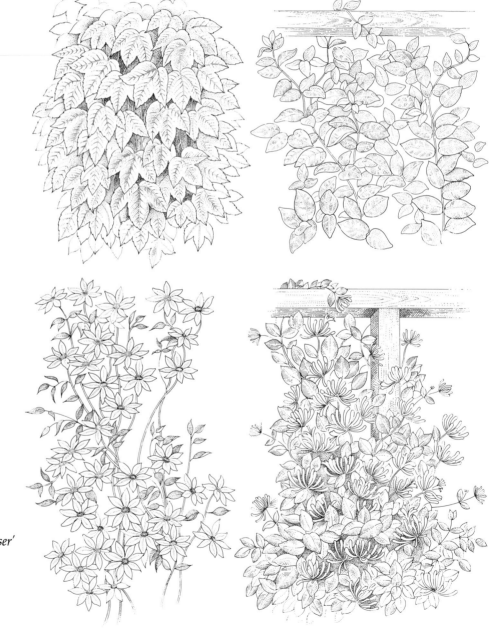

Left

Clematis 'Nelly Moser'

Right

Lonicera Americana

Name	Comments	US Hardiness zone
Ampelopsis brevipedunculata 'Elegans'	Non-vigorous ornamental vine good for restricted space; beautiful leaves with silver and pink variegation.	4
Clematis Jackmanii	Clematis need support around which to curl their leaf stalks. Good on a tree or large shrub. Jackmanii has violet-purple flowers June/Sept.	4–5
Nelly Moser	White striped carmine red, flowers May/June and Sept. East, south or west aspect.	4–5
montana rubens	Very vigorous; good for fast cover of shed etc. Single pink flowers May/June.	5
Fremontodendron californicum 'Californian Glory'	Fast growing evergreen makes a handsome plant with brilliant yellow flowers like large buttercups all summer. Sheltered south-facing position essential.	
Hedera canariensis 'Variegata'	Large-leaved ivy, quite vigorous.	7
helix 'Goldheart'	Moderate grower with neat, clinging habit and exquisite leaves variegated gold.	5
hibernica	'Irish ivy'; a vigorous climber with large dark green leaves. All ivies are evergreen.	5
Hydrangea petiolaris	Climbing hydrangea is self-clinging and useful for north and east facing positions. Lovely white flowers June/July.	4
Jasminum nudiflorum	Winter jasmine is vigorous and easy to grow. Yellow flowers November to March before leaves appear.	5
officinale 'Grandiflorum'	Scented white flowers in summer. Twining habit; can reach considerable height and spread.	7
Lonicera japonica 'Aureo-reticulata'	Semi-evergreen honeysuckle not too vigorous; leaves veined yellow, scented yellow flowers June/August.	4
japonica 'Halliana'	Vigorous evergreen honeysuckle, sweetly scented white flowers June/October. Twiner good for pergola.	4
periclymenum 'Belgica'	Beautifully scented yellow/pink flowers. Useful in shade and for scrambling over tree trunk or shed.	4
Parthenocissus quinquefolia	'Virginia creeper'. Partially self-clinging, good for trees, walls etc. Brilliant autumn colour; vigorous.	3
Polygonum baldschuanicum	'Russian vine' — an amazingly fast grower can soon smother a fence or outhouse. White flowers July/October.	4
Pyracantha 'Orange Glow'	Spiny evergreen good for walls and fences. Vigorous growth; large bright orange berries autumn/winter.	5–6
rogersiana	Evergreen. Free branching with bright red berries.	
Rose	Numerous species and named varieties of old and new rambling and climbing roses available; good for trellis, walls, pergolas, fences. Some notable names are: 'Etoile de Hollande' (red climber) 'Zephirine Drouhin' (perfumed pink), 'Mermaid' (yellow), 'Madame Alfred Carriere' (fragrant, free-flowering white).	5
Vitis coignetiae	Very vigorous self-supporting climber can be trained over walls, fences and into trees. Brilliant autumn leaf colour.	5
Wisteria sinensis	Climbs by twining; quite fast growing. Superb, sweetly scented hanging mauve flowers May/June. Needs sunny position.	5

Plants softening and complementing buildings and garden features: the clematis on the corner of a house (above) helps to blur the line where the house finishes and the garden begins, and contrasts well with the yellow flowers of Helichrysum angustifolium. Both combine with the staddle stone to form a satisfying composition.

Similarly the massed blue flowers of Ceanothus thyrsiflorus (opposite) enliven brick steps and foliage plants with a variety of leaf colour, shape and texture complement old York paving.

CONIFERS

Sizes shown give the likely height (and sometimes spread) after ten years in average conditions. For taller and faster growing conifers the ultimate sizes are also given.

SILVER GREY FOLIAGE

Name	Comments	Height
Chamaecyparis lawsoniana 'Columnaris Glauca'	Columnar habit.	10 ft (3 m) UH 25–30 ft (7.6–9 m)
'Pembury Blue'	Silvery–blue foliage.	8 ft (2.4 m) UH 25–30 ft (7.6–9 m)
Juniperus chinensis 'Blaauw's Variety'	Dense blue–grey foliage.	3 × 3 ft (90 × 90 cm)
'Pyramidalis'	Vividly glaucous juvenile foliage.	6 ft 6 in (2 m) UH 10–12 ft (3–3.5 m)
horizontalis 'Glauca'	Prostrate. Blue–green foliage.	6 in × 10 ft (15 cm × 3 m)
'Wiltonii'	Prostrate. Silvery–blue foliage.	4 in × 6 ft (10 cm × 2 m)
squamata 'Blue Carpet'	Intense silver–blue foliage.	8–12 in × 6 ft 6 in (20–30 cm × 2 m) spreading
'Blue Star'	Bright steel–blue foliage.	12 × 20 in (30 × 50 cm) spreading
'Meyeri'	Blue–grey dense foliage.	4 ft 6 in (1.4 m) UH 10–16 ft (3–4.5 m)
virginiana 'Grey Owl'	Fine grey foliage.	18–24 in × 6 ft 6 in (45–60 cm × 2 m) spreading
'Skyrocket'	Very narrow column, blue–grey.	6 ft 6 in (2 m) UH 20–25 ft (6–7.7 m)
Picea pungens glauca 'Koster'	Intense silvery–blue foliage.	8 ft (2.4 m) UH 25 ft (7.6 m)

GOLD FOLIAGE

Name	Comments	Height
Chamaecyparis lawsoniana 'Ellwoods Gold'	Foliage tinged yellow.	4 ft (1.2 m) slow growing
'Lanei Aurea'	Dense golden foliage.	6 ft 6 in (2 m) UH 35–50 ft (10–15 m)
'Minima Aurea'	Soft golden foliage.	1 ft (30 cm) UH 4 ft (1.2 m)
'Stewartii Erecta'	Bright yellow foliage.	8 ft (2.4 m) UH 35–50 ft (10–15 m)
pisifera 'Plumosa Aurea Nana'	Bright yellow feathery foliage.	3 ft (90 cm)
'Sungold'	Thread-like, overlapping branchlets of golden yellow.	2 ft (60 cm)
Juniperus communis 'Depressa Aurea'	Golden foliage in summer.	18 in × 4 ft (45 × 120 cm) spreading
media 'Old Gold'	Golden foliage all year.	3 × 4 ft (90 × 120 cm) spreading

116

Name	Comments	Height
'Pfitzeriana Aurea'	Branch tips golden yellow in summer.	4 × 6 ft (120 × 180 cm) UH 6 × 10–12 ft (1.8 × 3–3.5 m)
'Plumosa Aurea'	Foliage greenish bronze/yellow.	3 × 3 ft (90 × 90 cm) UH 10 × 10 ft (3 × 3 m)
Taxus baccata 'Fastigiata Aurea'	Deep yellow–green foliage.	5 ft (1.5 m) UH 13–16 ft (4–5 m)
'Semperaurea'	Foliage gold passing to rusty yellow.	3 × 3 ft (90 × 90 cm) spreading
'Standishii'	Rich golden yellow foliage.	3 ft (90 cm) slow growing
'Summergold'	Golden foliage, bright in summer.	18 in × 3 ft (45 × 90 cm) spreading
Thuya occidentalis 'Rheingold'	Old gold in summer, copper gold in winter.	3–4 ft (90–120 cm) UH 10 ft (3 m) variable
'Sunkist'	Bright gold all the year.	3–4 ft (90–120 cm)
orientalis 'Aurea Nana'	Golden yellow foliage in summer.	2 ft (60 cm) UH 5 ft (1.5 m)

GREEN FOLIAGE

Name	Comments	Height
Chamaecyparis lawsoniana 'Allumii'	Sea-green foliage. Good as specimen or hedge.	6 ft 6 in (2 m) UH 35–50 ft (10–15 m)
'Ellwoodii'	Grey–green feathery foliage. Compact pyramid shape.	6 ft 6 in (2 m) UH 16–20 ft (4.5–6 m)
'Kilmacurragh'	Narrow column of dark green.	6 ft 6 in (2 m) UH 35–50 ft (10–15 m)
'Minima Glauca'	Rounded cone of dense sea-green foliage. Slow.	1 ft (30 cm) UH 4 ft (120 cm)
Cryptomeria japonica 'Vilmoriniana'	Neat globular bush. Slow.	1 ft (30 cm) UH 4 ft (120 cm)
Juniperus horizontalis 'Emerald Spreader'	Flat, ground-hugging habit.	spread 5 ft (1.5 m)
'Hughes'	Grey–green foliage, ascending branches.	1 × 4 ft (30 × 120 cm)
media 'Mint Julep'	Rich, mint green, arching branches.	2 ft 6 in × 4 ft (80 × 120 cm)
'Pfitzeriana'	Strong growing, spreading.	3 × 6 ft 6 in (90 cm × 2 m) UH 7 × 10 ft (2.2 × 3 m)
Picea glauca 'Albertiana Conica'	Slow growing, dense conical shape.	3 ft (90 cm)
Taxus baccata 'Fastigiata' (Irish yew)	Deep green, upright shape.	6 ft (1.8 m)
Thuya occidentalis 'Smaragd'	Emerald green pyramid. Good for hedging.	8 ft (2.4 m) UH 20 ft (6 m)

US HARDINESS ZONE RATINGS

Name	Zone	Name	Zone
Chamaecyparis lawsoniana (all varieties)	5	Chamaecyparis pisifera (all varieties)	3
Juniperus chinensis (all varieties)	4	Juniperus communis	2
Juniperus horizontalis (all varieties)	3	Juniperus media (all varieties)	4
Juniperus squamata (all varieties)	4	Taxus baccata (all varieties)	6
Juniperus virginiana (all varieties)	2	Thuya occidentalis (all varieties)	2
Picea pungens & Picea glauca	2	Thuya orientalis	5 or 6
Cryptomeria japonica	5 or 6		

Pinus mugo

Perennials

Perennial plants include some of the loveliest and most familiar garden flowers. They form a permanent feature of planting schemes but are dormant during winter months, and so lend themselves very well to being combined with shrubs which can take over as interesting features at the coldest time of year. Like shrubs, perennials can be useful as high-points or 'fillers' in a border or they can spill softly over the front of the bed right down to ground level. They are most effective when planted in groups and although many like full sun, plants like hostas and bergenias thrive in damp shade.

All the perennial plants listed are normally hardy in the UK and most perennials are hardy in all parts of the USA; in the south and in western states some never become fully dormant.

Sizes are indicated as a general guide
small = up to 3 ft (90 cm)
medium = 3–6 ft (90–180cm)
large = 6 ft plus (180 cm)

Name	Comments	Height
Acanthus spinosus	Handsome plants of 'architectural' merit. Evergreen.	small
Achillea in variety (yarrow)	Yellow or white flowers June/August	small
Agapanthus in variety (African lily)	Feed and mulch well.	small
Ajuga in variety	Excellent flat ground covers with colourful foliage topped by short blue flower spikes in May/June. Evergreen.	small
Alchemilla mollis (lady's mantle)	Downy foliage.	small
Alstroemeria aurantica (herb lily)	Deep rooting. Orange flowers.	small
Alyssum saxatile 'Compactum'	Golden yellow, greyish foliage.	small
Anaphalis triplinervis	Woolly grey domes. 'Everlasting' flowers.	small
Artemisia 'Silver Queen' (wormwood)	Dainty, silvery divided foliage.	small
Asphodeline luteus	Glaucous green leaves; spikes of yellow flowers.	small
Bergenia	Rounded, glossy leaves, excellent ground cover. Evergreen.	small
Caltha palustris 'Plena'	Double 'king-cups' in spring. Rounded leaves.	small
Catananche coerulea 'Major'	Blue 'daisies' on wiry stalks.	small
Centaurea dealbata 'John Coutts'	Pink 'sweet sultan' flowers June/October.	small
Ceratostigma plumbaginoides	Plumbago blue flowers August/September.	small
Crambe cordifolia	Noble plants; huge leaves and flower 'clouds'.	medium

Name	Comments	Height
Crocosmia 'Lucifer'	Flame-red 'trumpets' in wands.	small
Dianthus in variety	Sweetly scented 'pinks' in various sizes.	small
Echinops ritro (globe thistle)	Blue heads; greyish leaves.	medium
Euphorbia myrsinites	Trailing stems; glaucous grey leaves. Evergreen.	small
Geranium in variety	Densely leafed. Free flowering.	small
Gunnera manicata	Leaves resemble gigantic rhubarb.	large
Gypsophila	Deeply rooted, they grow vigorously.	medium
Helianthemum in variety (sun rose)	Very colourful.	small
Helleborus in variety	Handsome foliage plants, provide excellent ground cover. Freely flowering in winter/early spring. Evergreen.	small
Holcus mollis 'Variegatus'	Buff-striped blades of grass.	small
Hosta in variety (plantain lily)	Clumps of broad, striking foliage are weed proof. Mauvish lily-like flowers July/August.	small
Incarvillea delavayi (trumpet flower)	May/June flowering.	small
Iberis 'Snowflake' (candytuft)	White flowers April/June. Evergreen.	small
Iris germanica in variety (bearded iris)	Iris enjoys hot sites with good drainage. June flowering. Evergreen.	medium
foetidissima	Yellow flowers; bright red seeds later. Evergreen.	small
pallida 'Variegata'	Glaucous and yellow striped foliage. Evergreen.	small
unguicularis (stylosa)	A winter gem; sun and poor soil. Evergreen.	small
Kniphofia in variety (red hot pokers)	August/October flowering.	medium
Liatris 'Kobold'	Mauvish spikes. Likes good drainage.	small
Libertia formosa	'Grassy' leaves. White flowers May/July.	small
Nepeta mussinii (catmint)	Blue flowers; grey foliage. Evergreen.	small
Nerine bowdenii	Pink 'trumpets' October/November. Likes shelter.	small
Oenothera in variety (evening primrose)	July/August.	small
Papaver orientale (oriental poppy)	Brilliantly coloured flowers.	small to medium
Penstemon barbatus (bearded tongue)	Pink spikes June/September.	small
Phlox subulata varieties	Alpine phlox flower freely in spring.	small
Potentilla in variety (cinquefoil)	Colourful flowers. Good ground cover.	small
Pulmonaria in variety	Early flowering ground coverers.	small
Pulsatilla vulgaris (pasque flower)	Violet purple bells April/May.	small
Rheum palmatum 'Rubrum'	Deeply lobed purplish leaves. Deep pinkish red flowers on spikes June/July.	medium

Hosta

Name	Comments	Height and spread
Saponaria ocymoides	Trailing plants, pink flowers May.	small
Sedum in variety (stonecrop)	Fleshy leafed, tolerates dry sites.	small
Sisyrinchium striatum	Grey–green tufts of foliage. Evergreen.	small
Stachys	Easy ground coverers with grey foliage. Evergreen.	small
Stipa	Ornamental grasses with attractive foliage.	medium
Thymus in variety (thyme)	Form dense mats.	small
Trollius in variety (globe flower)	Yellow or orange buttercup-like flowers May/June.	small
Verbascum in variety (mullein)	Thrives on chalk. Yellow flower spikes.	medium to large
Viola hederacea	Good ground cover. Flowers all summer.	small
Zauschneria californica	Scarlet flowers, grey leaves.	small

Bulbs for Landscaping

Growing bulb flowers in your garden need not mean planting those bright, showy specimens every autumn, along with the attendant chores of lifting, drying, cleaning and storing if they are to be used again next year. Instead, there are very many spring and summer flowering bulbs—most, but not all, being species or less horticulturally developed cultivars—that, once planted can be left undisturbed in the garden to naturalise, where they will flower as part of the permanent planting scheme for several years. Indeed, when happily settled they are likely to spread and multiply.

These year-round bulbs for landscaping thrive in sunny or partially shaded sites and can be 'naturalised' in almost any location that is not seasonally dug over—in plant borders with shrubs and perennials, under a solitary tree, in lawns, on grassy slopes, in rough grass, among rocks or along walls, as well as in containers where they combine well with shrubs.

Bulbs for landscaping should be planted after all other plants are in place. Position them in groups and drifts of 'natural' appearance, to look as if they had emerged from natural offsets or seeds, but ensure that the bulbs do not touch and that the flowers will have breathing space when they emerge. In grass, bulb foliage should be allowed to wither before the grass is mown and in all situations naturalised bulbs will benefit from an annual application of bonemeal.

This approach to growing bulbs is well worth a try, if only because they are such easy plants, giving much reward in the way of colour and perfume for such little effort.

All the bulbs suitable for landscaping are normally hardy in the USA.

Perennial Irises growing in water in Koishikawa Gardens, Tokyo, Japan.

Name	Comments	Height
Agapanthus (Headbourne hybrids)	Various blues flowering July/September.	2–3 ft (60–90 cm)
Allium (all species)	White, yellow to purples flowering May/July.	6–48 in (15–120 cm)
Amaryllis belladonna	Fragrant, pale rose pink, September/October.	2–2½ ft (60–75 cm)
Anemone appenina	Sky blue, March/April.	6 in (15 cm)
blanda and cultivars	Wide range of colours, March.	4–5 in (10–12 cm)
nemorosa	White, tinged pink, May.	6 in (15 cm)
Brodiaea lactea	White, flushed lilac, June.	18–24 in (45–60 cm)
laxa	Dark blue, June/July.	18–20 in (45–50 cm)
'Queen Fabiola'	Blue–violet, June/July.	18–20 in (45–50 cm)
tubergenii	Pale and dark blue, July.	18 in (45 cm)
Camassia cusickii	Wisteria blue, June/July.	2 ft (60 cm)
esculenta	Violet, May/June.	3 ft (90 cm)
leichtlinii 'Caerulea'	Aster blue, June/July.	3 ft (90 cm)

Corylus avellana 'Contorta' can be underplanted with snowdrops or Iris reticulata

Name	Comments	Height
Chionodoxa gigantea	Gentian blue, April.	10 in (25 cm)
luciliae	Porcelain blue, March/April.	4–6 in (10–15 cm)
'Pink Giant'	Rosy-pink, March/April.	6 in (15 cm)
sardensis	Royal blue, March.	4–6 in (10–15 cm)
Colchicum (all species and Dutch hybrids)	Wide range, August/November.	6–8 in (15–20 cm)
Convallaria majalis	Fragrant, pure white, April/June.	9 in (22 cm)
Corydalis solida	Cream to purple, April.	6 in (15 cm)
Crinum powellii and album	Rose pink and white, July/September.	3½ ft (105 cm)
Crocosmia (all species and hybrids—Montbretia)	Red, yellow, oranges and scarlet, July/September.	20–36 in (50–90 cm)
Crocus (all spring flowering species and Dutch hybrids)	Various shades and striped, feathered and stippled, January/April.	3 in (8 cm)
(all autumn flowering species)	White, blues, lilac, September – February	3–4 in (8–10 cm)
Cyclamen (most autumn flowering species)	White, pink, July/October.	3 in (8 cm)
(most spring flowering species)	Roses, purples, January/May.	2–4 in (5–10 cm)
Eranthis cilica	Deep yellow, February.	4–5 in (10–12 cm)
hyemalis	Golden yellow, January/February.	3 in (8 cm)
tubergenii	Large golden yellow, February/March.	5 in (12 cm)
Eremurus (all species and hybrids)	Wide range of colours, June/July	2–6 ft (60–180 cm)
Erythronium (all species and hybrids)	Wide range of colours, March/May.	4–12 in (10–30 cm)

Name	Comments	Height
Fritillaria imperials and hybrids	Yellow, orange, red, April/May.	26–36 in (65–90 cm)
meleagris and hybrids	White to violet chequered, April/May.	10–12 in (25–30 cm)
persica	Greenish–mauve to purple, April/May.	3–4 ft (90–120 cm)
Galanthus elwesii	Pearly white, February.	7 in (17 cm)
nivalis simplex	Snow white, January/February.	6 in (15 cm)
nivalis flore pleno	Double form, January/February.	6 in (15 cm)
nivalis 'S. Arnott'	Fragrant, white, February.	10 in (25 cm)
Galtonia candicans	Fragrant, pure white, July/August.	3–4 ft (90–120 cm)
Incarvillea delavayi	Rosy–carmine, May/July.	1–1½ ft (30–45 cm)
Iris danfordiae	Fragrant lemon yellow, February.	3 in (8 cm)
histrioides major	Fragrant, gentian blue, March.	3 in (8 cm)
reticulata and hybrids	Fragrant, various blue and purples, February/March.	4–6 in (10–15 cm)
Leucojum aestivum	White, tipped green, May/June.	18 in (45 cm)
'Gravetye Giant'	Larger, white form, May/June.	2 ft (60 cm)
vernum	White, tipped green, February/March.	6 in (15 cm)
Lilium—most cultivars but specially recommended are		
amabile	Rich red, July.	2–3 ft (60–90 cm)
hansonii	Fragrant, golden yellow, June.	3 ft (90 cm)
henryi	Orange spotted deep brown, August/September.	7 ft (210 cm)
martagon	Usually purple–pink, June/July.	3 ft (90 cm)
pardalinum	Orange–yellow spotted red, July.	2½–4 ft (75–120 cm)
pumilum	Scarlet, June/July.	1½–2 ft (45–60 cm)
regale	White, flushed rose, July/August.	5 ft (150 cm)
speciosum	Fragrant, waxy white, spotted crimson, August/September.	5 ft (150 cm)
and all varieties	Fragrant, white, pink, carmine, August/September.	5 ft (150 cm)
all American hybrids	Yellow, orange, red, July.	3–6 ft (90–180 cm)
all Asiatic hybrids	White, orange, yellow, red, June/July.	20–48 in (50–120 cm)
all Oriental hybrids	White, crimson, August/September.	4–5 ft (120–150 cm)
Muscari armeniacum	Fragrant, deep cobalt blue, April.	6–8 in (15–20 cm)
'Blue Spike'	Fragrant, flax blue, April.	6 in (15 cm)
azureum	Bright blue, March.	6 in (15 cm)
botryoides album	Fragrant, white, March/April.	6–10 in (15–25 cm)
tubergenianum	Bright deep blue, April/May.	8 in (20 cm)
Narcissus—most cultivars but species, cyclamineus hybrids and others specially recommended are:		
bulbocodium var. conspicuus	Golden yellow, March.	6 in (15 cm)
cyclamineus	Golden yellow, February/March.	6 in (15 cm)
'February Gold'	Clear yellow, February/March.	12 in (30 cm)
'March Sunshine'	Yellow and orange, March.	10 in (25 cm)

125

Mahonia japonica (detail) can be complemented by a group of Muscari or Narcissus

Name	Comments	Height
'Jack Snipe'	White and yellow, March.	9 in (22 cm)
'Jenny'	Pure white, March/April.	10 in (25 cm)
'Peeping Tom'	Rich yellow, March/April.	14 in (35 cm)
'Tete a Tete'	Lemon yellow, February/March.	8 in (20 cm)
lobularis	White and yellow, February/March.	7 in (17 cm)
tazetta hybrid 'Minnow'	Soft to deep yellow, March.	7 in (17 cm)
triandrus albus	White, March.	7 in (17 cm)
poeticus 'Actea'	White and scarlet, April.	17 in (40 cm)
Ornithogalum nutans	White touched green, April/May.	9–12 in (22–30 cm)
umbellatum	White, May/June.	6 in (15 cm)
Puschkinia libanotica	Silvery–blue, March/April.	6 in (15 cm)
alba	Pure white, March/April.	6 in (15 cm)
Scilla campanulata	Blue, pink, white, May.	12–18 in (30–45 cm)
nutans	Fragrant, violet blue, May.	10–12 in (25–30 cm)
siberica	Prussian blue, March/April.	4 in (10 cm)
alba	White, March/April.	4 in (10 cm)
'Spring Beauty'	Sky blue, March/April.	6–8 in (15–20 cm)
tubergeniana	Soft, silvery–blue, February/March.	4 in (10 cm)
Sternbergia lutea	Clear yellow, August/October.	4–6 in (10–15 cm)
macrantha	Bright yellow, September/October.	4–6 in (10–15 cm)
Triteleia uniflora	Fragrant. Lilac blue, March/May.	4–6 in (10–15 cm)
'Wisley Blue'	Violet blue, March/May.	4 in (10 cm)

Tulipa—only species and kaufmaniana hybrids can be naturalised in grass, but fosteriana and greigii hybrids, 'Triumph' and 'Single Late' varieties can be most effectively used in landscape constructions. There is a multicoloured choice in more colours than the rainbow.

HEDGES

Name	Comments	Planting distance
LOW GROWING HEDGES		
These do not normally grow to more than 3–4 ft (1–1.2 m).		
Berberis thunbergii 'Atropurpurea Nana'	Reddish–purple leaves	14 in (35 cm)
Hebe anomala	White flowers. Evergreen.	$1\frac{1}{2}$ ft (45 cm)
Lavandula spica (old English lavender)	Grey foliage. Scented.	$1\frac{1}{2}$ ft (45 cm)
Potentilla fruticosa 'Farreri'	Yellow flowers all summer.	2 ft (60 cm)
Prunus cistena Crimson Dwarf	Crimson leaves, pink flowers.	2 ft (60 cm)
FORMAL FOLIAGE HEDGES		
Carpinus (hornbeam)	Avoid heavy, wet soils	$1\frac{1}{2}$ ft (45 cm)
Crataegus (quickthorn)	Can be planted alone or mixed with beech, hornbeam, privet etc.	1 ft (30 cm)
Fagus (beech) green or purple	Avoid heavy, wet soils.	$1\frac{1}{2}$ ft (45 cm)
Ligustrum (privet) common golden oval leaf	The golden and oval leaf are semi-evergreen.	1 ft (30 cm)
INFORMAL FLOWERING AND FOLIAGE HEDGES		
Berberis thunbergii 'Erecta'	Good autumn colour, narrow upright growth.	$1\frac{1}{2}$ ft (45 cm)
Cotoneaster simonsii	Colourful leaves and berries. Semi-evergreen.	$1\frac{1}{2}$ ft (45 cm)

Berberis thunbergii 'Atropurpurea Nana'

Name	Comments	Planting distance
Ilex (holly)	Makes a good dense hedge.	1½ ft (45 cm)
Lonicera nitida	Black berries. Evergreen.	2 ft (60 cm)
Prunus laurocerasus 'Rotundifolia' (laurel)	Light green leaves. Evergreen.	2 ft (60 cm)

FLOWERING AND BERRYING HEDGES

Name	Comments	Planting distance
Berberis stenophylla	Yellow flowers. Prune after flowering. Evergreen.	2 ft (60 cm)
Escallonia	Prune lightly in spring. Semi-evergreen.	2½ ft (75 cm)
Pyracantha rogersiana	White flowers; red berries. Evergreen.	20 in (50 cm)
Rhododendron ponticum (common rhododendron)	Purplish pink flowers. Large hedge unsuitable for chalky soil.	3 ft (90 cm)

ROSES
Name	Comments	Planting distance
Shrub and old-fashioned species roses	Cut out dead wood in March.	varies according to variety. Check when buying plants
Symphoricarpus 'Magic Berry'	Lilac carmine berries.	3 ft (90 cm)

CONIFER HEDGES
Name	Comments	Planting distance
Chamaecyparis lawsoniana 'Allumii'	Bluish–grey.	2 ft (60 cm)
Cupressocyparis leylandii	Grey–green; fast growing.	2½ ft (75 cm)
Thuya plicata 'Atrovirens'	Bright green. Trim with secateurs in summer.	2 ft (60 cm)
Taxux baccata (yew)	Trim late in summer.	1½–2 ft (45–60 cm)

NOTE FOR US READERS: GUIDE TO HEDGING PLANTS THAT DO NOT APPEAR IN OTHER LISTS (SHRUBS OR CONIFERS)

Name	Zone	Name	Zone
Berberis thunbergii	4	Lonicera nitida	3
Crataegus	4	Ligustrum	3
Carpinus	4	Prunus cistena	2
Fagus	4		

Ground Cover

GROUND COVER PLANTS FOR A PURPOSE

* = safe to plant, —— = avoid for the condition indicated.

Low Growing, Carpeting Subjects which help to exclude weeds and reduce work to the minimum. These rarely exceed 3 ft (1 m) in height. To achieve the best results both visually and in excluding weeds, they should be planted in bold drifts and clumps.

Subject	Loamy Soil	Limy Soil	Clay Soil	Dry Sunny Sites	Dry Shady Sites	Moist Shady Sites	Maritime Areas
Acaena	*	*	—	*	—	—	*
Acanthus	*	*	*	*	*	—	—
Ajuga	*	*	*	—	—	*	—
Alchemilla	*	*	*	—	*	*	*
Alyssum	*	*	—	*	—	—	*
Anaphalis	*	*	—	*	*	—	—
Anchusa	*	*	—	—	—	—	—
Anemone	*	*	*	—	—	—	—
Anthemis	*	—	—	*	—	—	—
Arctostaphylos uva-ursi	*	—	—	*	*	*	—
Armeria	*	*	—	*	—	—	*
Artemisia	*	—	—	*	*	—	*
Astrantia	—	—	*	—	—	*	—
Aubrieta	*	*	*	*	—	—	*
Berberis low	*	*	*	—	*	—	*
Bergenia	*	*	*	—	—	*	*
Brunnera	*	*	*	—	*	—	*

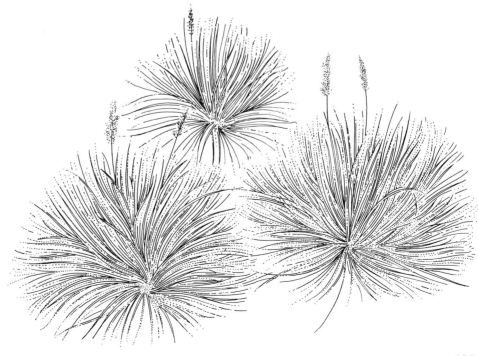

Festuca glauca

Subject	Loamy Soil	Limy Soil	Clay Soil	Dry Sunny Sites	Dry Shady Sites	Moist Shady Sites	Maritime Areas
Caltha	*	*	*	—	—	*	—
Campanula	*	*	—	—	—	—	*
Ceanothus repens	*	—	—	—	—	—	—
Centaurea	*	*	—	*	—	—	*
Ceratostigma	*	*	—	*	—	—	*
Chaenomeles	*	*	*	*	—	—	—
Cistus	*	*	—	*	—	—	*
Convolvulus	*	*	—	*	—	—	*
Cotoneaster	*	*	*	*	*	—	—
Dianthus	*	*	—	*	—	—	*
Dicentra	*	—	—	—	—	—	—
Epimedium	*	*	*	*	*	*	—
Erica	*	—	—	—	—	—	*
Erigeron	*	*	—	—	—	—	—
Eryngium	*	—	—	—	—	—	*
Euonymus fortunei forms	*	*	*	—	—	—	*
Euphorbia	*	*	—	—	*	—	*
Festuca	*	*	—	*	*	—	*
Fuchsia	*	*	—	—	—	—	*
Gaultheria	*	—	—	—	—	—	—
Genista hispanica	*	*	—	*	—	—	*
Geranium	*	*	*	*	*	—	*
Hebe	*	*	—	*	—	—	*
Hedera	*	*	*	*	*	—	*
Helianthemum	*	*	—	*	—	—	*
Helleborus	*	*	*	—	—	—	—
Hemerocallis	*	*	*	—	—	*	*
Heuchera	*	—	—	—	*	—	*
Hosta	*	—	*	—	—	*	*
Hypericum androsaemum	*	*	*	*	*	—	*
calycinum	*	*	*	*	*	—	*
Iberis	*	—	—	*	—	—	*

Spiraea bumalda

Subject	Loamy Soil	Limy Soil	Clay Soil	Dry Sunny Sites	Dry Shady Sites	Moist Shady Sites	Maritime Areas
Iris foetidissima	*	*	—	—	*	—	*
Juniperus media	*	*	—	*	—	—	*
Lamium	*	*	*	—	*	—	*
Lavandula	*	*	—	*	*	—	*
Liriope	*	*	—	—	*	—	*
Lonicera pileata	*	*	*	—	—	—	*
Lysimachia	*	—	—	—	—	*	—
Mahonia	*	*	*	*	*	—	*
Nepeta	*	*	—	*	—	—	—
Omphalodes	*	—	—	—	*	—	—
Osmanthus	*	*	—	—	—	—	—
Pachysandra	*	—	—	—	*	—	—
Phlomis	*	*	—	*	*	—	—
Phlox—alpine forms	*	—	—	—	—	—	*
Polygonatum	*	*	*	—	*	*	—
Polygonum	*	*	*	—	*	*	*
Potentilla	*	*	—	*	—	—	*
Primula	*	*	—	—	—	*	—
Prunus Zabelliana	*	*	*	—	*	—	—
Pulmonaria	*	*	—	*	*	*	—
Pulsatilla	*	*	—	—	—	—	*
Ruta	*	—	—	*	—	—	*
Salix	*	—	*	—	—	*	—
Salvia	*	*	*	*	—	—	*
Santolina	*	*	*	*	—	—	*
Saponaria	*	—	*	*	—	—	—
Sarcococca	*	—	*	—	*	—	—
Saxifraga	*	—	—	—	—	—	—
Scabiosa	*	*	*	—	—	—	*
Sedum	*	*	*	*	—	—	*
Senecio	*	*	*	*	—	—	*
Spiraea japonica	*	*	*	—	—	—	*
Stachys	*	*	*	*	*	—	*
Symphoricarpus	*	*	*	*	*	—	*
Tellima	*	*	*	—	—	—	—
Teucrium	*	—	—	*	—	—	—
Thymus	*	*	*	*	—	—	*
Tiarella	*	—	—	—	*	—	—
Viburnum davidii	*	*	*	—	—	—	—
Vinca	*	*	*	*	*	—	*
Viola	*	*	*	*	—	—	*
Waldsteinia	*	*	*	—	*	*	—
Zauschneria	*	*	—	*	*	—	*

Note for US readers:
All perennials are normally hardy in all areas. Details of most shrubs are given in the separate general shrub list.

Acknowledgements

The authors and publishers would like to thank the following organizations and individuals for their help.

Photographers and photograph suppliers
Heather Angel pages 86, 87, 99, 106, 114 above, 115, 122; Bradstone Garden Products (G. Worrall) pages 34, 42, 55, 71, 75, 94 below; Cement and Concrete Association page 26; Fox Pools pages 64–5; Derek Goard pages 11, 23, 27, 43 above and below, 50 above and below, 51, 90, 91 above and below; Hozelock-ASL Ltd page 54; Practical Householder page 95; Practical Woodworking (Alan Mitchell) pages 30 above and below; Graham Richardson title page, pages 10, 14, 15 above and below, 18, 19 above and below, 22, 58 above and below, 59, 66, 67 above and below, 70 above and below, 74 above and below, 78, 79 above and below, 82 above and below, 94 above, 114 below; John Sandall page 35.

Designers and exhibitors of gardens
Geoff and Faith Whiten for Halifax Building Society pages 18, 19 above and below, 23, 42, 43 above and below, 58 above and below, 59, 70 above and below, 74 below, 83; Geoff and Faith Whiten pages 26, 27, 30 above and below, 31, 34, 35, 54, 71, 75, 94 above and below, 95; Landscape students of Merrist Wood College pages 10, 11, 66, 67 above and below, 82 below; Peter Rogers pages 14, 15 above and below, 74 above, 82 above; Preben Jakobsen for A. Brophy Landscapes pages 78, 79 above and below; David Stevens for F. W. Woolworth page 22; Douglas Knight pages 90, 91 above and below; David Wassell for Telford Development Corporation pages 50 above and below, 51; above and F. W. Woolworth page 114 below.

Artwork
All garden designs drawn by Geoffrey Whiten, who is a member of the Society of Landscape and Garden Designers. All other artwork by Paul Saunders. The Hardiness Zones of North America (page 134) Copyright © 1985 The President and Fellows of Harvard College. Adapted from Arnoldia, the quarterly magazine of the Arnold Arboretum and used with permission.

Suppliers of plants and materials

Trees, shrubs, conifers, climbers and perennials listed can all be found in Notcutts Nurseries' comprehensive mail order catalogue, available from:
Notcutts Nurseries Ltd
Woodbridge
Suffolk IP12 4AF and are available from any of Notcutts garden centres in the UK south, east and midlands.

Bulbs, perennials, shrubs, climbers also available by mail order from:
Spalding Bulb Company
Spalding
Lincolnshire
and
Hortico,
Spalding,
Lincolnshire

Perennials and shrubs, especially Phormiums:
Bressingham Gardens
Bressingham
Diss
Norfolk IP22 2AB

Paving (Octavian, Corinium, Sets, Riven) and walling (Traditional, Hadrian, Cotswall, Aztec):
Bradstone Garden Products
ECC Quarries Ltd
Okus
Swindon
Wilts SN1 4JJ

Pond equipment and aquatic plants:
Stapeley Water Gardens Ltd
Stapeley
Nantwich
Cheshire CW5 7JA

Garden lights and submersible pumps:
Hozelock Ltd
Haddenham
Aylesbury
Buckinghamshire HP17 8JD

Chinese earthenware pots:
Brian Hamilton
Snapdragon
268 Lee High Road
London SE13

Terracotta pots:
C. H. Brannam Ltd
Litchdon Potteries
Barnstaple
Devon EX32 8NE

Sculpture:
Malcolm Pollard
42 East Park Parade
Northampton NN1 4LA

Pebbles and stone chippings:
Border Stone
Middleton Quarry
Middleton
Welshpool
Powys SY21 8DJ

Information on membership, horticultural advice and the Chelsea Show from
The Secretary,
The Royal Horticultural Society
Vincent Square
London SW1P 2PE

Useful addresses in the United States of America

American Society of Landscape Architects
1733 Connecticut Avenue NW
Washington DC 20009

Information on local and specialist retail nurseries from: American Association of Nurserymen
230 Southern Building
Washington DC 20005

Information on garden centres and other suppliers:
American Horticultural Society
Box 0105
Mount Vernon
Virginia 22121

Information on local garden clubs:
The Garden Club of America
598 Madison Avenue
New York
NY 10022

Hardiness Zones of North America

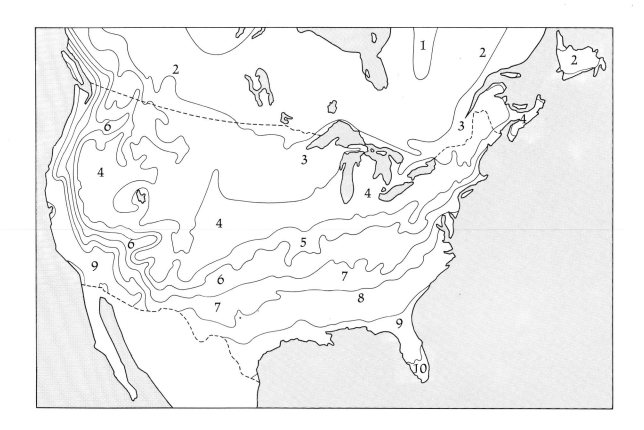

The limits of the average annual minimum temperatures for each zone.

Zone 1	below	−50°F	Zone 6	below	−5°− +5°
Zone 2		−50° −−35°	Zone 7		5°− 10°
Zone 3		−35° −−20°	Zone 8		10°− 20°
Zone 4		−20° −−10°	Zone 9		20°− 30°
Zone 5		−10° − −5°	Zone 10		30°− 40°

Compiled by the Arnold Arboretum, Harvard University, Jamaica Plain, Mass.

Note
Hardiness ratings give only a guide to conditions suitable for particular plants and should not be taken as the sole factor in choosing what to grow, especially if the garden has well-drained soil and shelter from wind.

Index

Italicised numerals refer either to captions or uncaptioned illustrations